Immigration to North America

Middle Eastern Immigrants

Ed Warms

Immigration to North America

Middle Eastern Immigrants

Ed Warms

Senior Consulting Editor Stuart Anderson
former Associate Commissioner for Policy and Planning,
US. Citizenship and Immigration Services

Introduction by Marian L. Smith, Historian,
U.S. Citizenship and Immigration Services

Introduction by Peter A. Hammerschmidt,
former First Secretary, Permanent Mission of Canada to the United Nations

MASON CREST
PHILADELPHIA

Mason Crest
450 Parkway Drive, Suite D
Broomall, PA 19008
www.masoncrest.com

©2017 by Mason Crest, an imprint of National Highlights, Inc.

Printed and bound in the United States of America.

CPSIA Compliance Information: Batch #INA2016.
For further information, contact Mason Crest at 1-866-MCP-Book.

First printing
1 3 5 7 9 8 6 4 2

Library of Congress Cataloging-in-Publication Data

on file at the Library of Congress
ISBN: 978-1-4222-3689-5 (hc)
ISBN: 978-1-4222-8106-2 (ebook)

Immigration to North America series ISBN: 978-1-4222-3679-6

Table of Contents

KEY ICONS TO LOOK FOR:

Words to Understand: These words with their easy-to-understand definitions will increase the reader's understanding of the text, while building vocabulary skills.

Sidebars: This boxed material within the main text allows readers to build knowledge, gain insights, explore possibilities, and broaden their perspectives by weaving together additional information to provide realistic and holistic perspectives.

Research Projects: Readers are pointed toward areas of further inquiry connected to each chapter. Suggestions are provided for projects that encourage deeper research and analysis.

Text-Dependent Questions: These questions send the reader back to the text for more careful attention to the evidence presented there.

Series Glossary of Key Terms: This back-of-the book glossary contains terminology used throughout this series. Words found here increase the reader's ability to read and comprehend higher-level books and articles in this field.

The Changing Face of the United States

Marian L. Smith, Historian
U.S. Citizenship and Immigration Services

Americans commonly assume that immigration today is very different than immigration of the past. The immigrants themselves appear to be unlike immigrants of earlier eras. Their language, their dress, their food, and their ways seem strange. At times people fear too many of these new immigrants will destroy the America they know. But has anything really changed? Do new immigrants have any different effect on America than old immigrants a century ago? Is the American fear of too much immigration a new development? Do immigrants really change America more than America changes the immigrants? The very subject of immigration raises many questions.

In the United States, immigration is more than a chapter in a history book. It is a continuous thread that links the present moment to the first settlers on North American shores. From the first colonists' arrival until today, immigrants have been met by Americans who both welcomed and feared them. Immigrant contributions were always welcome—on the farm, in the fields, and in the factories. Welcoming the poor, the persecuted, and the "huddled masses" became an American principle. Beginning with the original Pilgrims' flight from religious persecution in the 1600s, through the Irish migration to escape starvation in the 1800s, to the relocation of Central Americans seeking refuge from civil wars in the 1980s and 1990s, the United States has considered itself a haven for the destitute and the oppressed.

But there was also concern that immigrants would not adopt American ways, habits, or language. Too many immigrants might overwhelm America. If so, the dream of the Founding Fathers for United States government and society would be destroyed. For this reason, throughout American history some have argued that limiting or ending immigration is our patriotic duty. Benjamin Franklin feared there were so many German immigrants in Pennsylvania the Colonial Legislature would begin speaking German. "Progressive" leaders of the early 1900s feared that immigrants who could not read and understand the English language were not only exploited by "big business," but also served as the foundation for "machine politics" that undermined the U.S. Constitution. This theme continues today, usually voiced by those who bear no malice toward immigrants but who want to preserve American ideals.

Have immigrants changed? In colonial days, when most colonists were of English descent, they considered Germans, Swiss, and French immigrants as different. They were not "one of us" because they spoke a different language. Generations later, Americans of German or French descent viewed Polish, Italian, and Russian immigrants as strange. They were not "like us" because they had a different religion, or because they did not come from a tradition of constitutional government. Recently, Americans of Polish or Italian descent have seen Nicaraguan, Pakistani, or Vietnamese immigrants as too different to be included. It has long been said of American immigration that the latest ones to arrive usually want to close the door behind them.

It is important to remember that fear of individual immigrant groups seldom lasted, and always lessened. Benjamin Franklin's anxiety over German immigrants disappeared after those immigrants' sons and daughters helped the nation gain independence in the Revolutionary War. The Irish of the mid-1800s were among the most hated immigrants, but today we all wear green on St. Patrick's Day. While a century ago it was feared that Italian and other Catholic immigrants would vote as directed by the Pope, today that controversy is only a vague memory. Unfortunately, some ethnic groups continue their efforts to earn acceptance. The African

Americans' struggle continues, and some Asian Americans, whose families have been in America for generations, are the victims of current anti-immigrant sentiment.

Time changes both immigrants and America. Each wave of new immigrants, with their strange language and habits, eventually grows old and passes away. Their American-born children speak English. The immigrants' grandchildren are completely American. The strange foods of their ancestors—spaghetti, baklava, hummus, or tofu—become common in any American restaurant or grocery store. Much of what the immigrants brought to these shores is lost, principally their language. And what is gained becomes as American as St. Patrick's Day, Hanukkah, or Cinco de Mayo, and we forget that it was once something foreign.

Recent immigrants are all around us. They come from every corner of the earth to join in the American Dream. They will continue to help make the American Dream a reality, just as all the immigrants who came before them have done.

Welcome to the
United States
A Guide for New
Immigrants

UNITED STATES OF AMERICA   Department of Homeland Security

PERMANENT RESIDENT CARD

 UNITED STATES OF AME

We recommend you use this env
protect your new card.

The Changing Face of Canada

Peter A. Hammerschmidt
former First Secretary, Permanent Mission of Canada to the United Nations

Throughout Canada's history, immigration has shaped and defined the very character of Canadian society. The migration of peoples from every part of the world into Canada has profoundly changed the way we look, speak, eat, and live. Through close and distant relatives who left their lands in search of a better life, all Canadians have links to immigrant pasts. We are a nation built by and of immigrants.

Two parallel forces have shaped the history of Canadian immigration. The enormous diversity of Canada's immigrant population is the most obvious. In the beginning came the enterprising settlers of the "New World," the French and English colonists. Soon after came the Scottish, Irish, and Northern and Central European farmers of the 1700s and 1800s. As the country expanded westward during the mid-1800s, migrant workers began arriving from China, Japan, and other Asian countries. And the turbulent twentieth century brought an even greater variety of immigrants to Canada, from the Caribbean, Africa, India, and Southeast Asia.

So while English- and French-Canadians are the largest ethnic groups in the country today, neither group alone represents a majority of the population. A large and vibrant multicultural mix makes up the rest, particularly in Canada's major cities. Toronto, Vancouver, and Montreal alone are home to people from over 200 ethnic groups!

Less obvious but equally important in the evolution of Canadian immigration has been hope. The promise of a better life lured Europeans and

Americans seeking cheap (sometimes even free) farmland. Thousands of Scots and Irish arrived to escape grinding poverty and starvation. Others came for freedom, to escape religious and political persecution. Canada has long been a haven to the world's dispossessed and disenfranchised—Dutch and German farmers cast out for their religious beliefs, black slaves fleeing the United States, and political refugees of despotic regimes in Europe, Africa, Asia, and South America.

The two forces of diversity and hope, so central to Canada's past, also shaped the modern era of Canadian immigration. Following the Second World War, Canada drew heavily on these influences to forge trailblazing immigration initiatives.

The catalyst for change was the adoption of the Canadian Bill of Rights in 1960. Recognizing its growing diversity and Canadians' changing attitudes towards racism, the government passed a federal statute barring discrimination on the grounds of race, national origin, color, religion, or sex. Effectively rejecting the discriminatory elements in Canadian immigration policy, the Bill of Rights forced the introduction of a new policy in 1962. The focus of immigration abruptly switched from national origin to the individual's potential contribution to Canadian society. The door to Canada was now open to every corner of the world.

Welcoming those seeking new hopes in a new land has also been a feature of Canadian immigration in the modern era. The focus on economic immigration has increased along with Canada's steadily growing economy, but political immigration has also been encouraged. Since 1945, Canada has admitted tens of thousands of displaced persons, including Jewish Holocaust survivors, victims of Soviet crackdowns in Hungary and Czechoslovakia, and refugees from political upheaval in Uganda, Chile, and Vietnam.

Prior to 1978, however, these political refugees were admitted as an exception to normal immigration procedures. That year, Canada revamped its refugee policy with a new Immigration Act that explicitly affirmed Canada's commitment to the resettlement of refugees from oppression. Today, the admission of refugees remains a central part of

Canadian immigration law and regulations.

Amendments to economic and political immigration policy have continued, refining further the bold steps taken during the modern era. Together, these initiatives have turned Canada into one of the world's few truly multicultural states.

Unlike the process of assimilation into a "melting pot" of cultures, immigrants to Canada are more likely to retain their cultural identity, beliefs, and practices. This is the source of some of Canada's greatest strengths as a society. And as a truly multicultural nation, diversity is not seen as a threat to Canadian identity. Quite the contrary—diversity is Canadian identity.

1 A MOSAIC OF DIVERSITY

Like a tile mosaic, the Middle East is one large, complex picture made up of many small and unique pieces. The presence of Arabs and non-Arabs; Muslims, Christians, and Jews; and Kurds, Berbers, and other ethnic groups adds shades of color to (and often overshadows) national affiliations. The distinctions sometimes blur. For example, some Arabs are Christians, and many Arab countries are also home to small Jewish communities. Iran and Turkey—among the most populous countries in the region—are not Arab at all. Kurds and Palestinians, two peoples without a homeland, are scattered throughout various Middle Eastern countries.

Not even the definition of the Middle East is set in stone. Some people use the term in a strictly geographic sense, to denote the countries of southwest Asia and northeastern Africa; for others, the Middle East is a political designation that also includes all the predominantly Muslim countries in North Africa. As used in this book, the term *Middle East* will include Algeria, Bahrain, Egypt, Iraq, Jordan, Kuwait, Lebanon, Libya, Morocco, Oman, Qatar, Saudi Arabia, Sudan, Syria, Tunisia, the United Arab Emirates, Yemen, and the Palestinians—all the members of the Arab League with the exception of Somalia, Mauritania, Djibouti, and Comoros, which are actually not Arab countries—as well as Iran, Israel, and Turkey.

◄ The Middle East comprises a multitude of peoples and cultures. The crowd in this 2001 photo has assembled in Jerusalem to demonstrate for peace between Palestinians and Israelis.

Given the ethnic and cultural diversity of these countries, it should come as no surprise that there is no "typical" Middle Eastern American or Canadian. The Arab American community, in particular, has diversified. In *Arabs in America: Building a New Future*, author Lisa Suhair Majaj observes:

> In contrast to the earlier Arab immigrant population, composed largely of Christians from Mount Lebanon, the current Arab-American community is far from homogenous. It includes people of many different national origins and religions; recent immigrants and assimilated descendants of earlier immigrants; dark-skinned and light-skinned individuals; people who speak no Arabic, those who speak no English, and those whose dialects are unintelligible to each other; and children of mixed marriages whose hybrid identities locate them at the margins of "Arab" and "American" identity.

Middle Easterners have lived in North America since the late 1800s. But changes in immigration policy have increased the numbers of Middle Eastern people able to enter the United States or Canada. In the United States, the landmark legislation was the Immigration Act of 1965, which removed "national origin" quotas that severely limited the number of Middle Easterners, Asians, certain southern Europeans, and other ethnic groups who could

 Words to Understand in This Chapter

asylum—protection given by a country to people who have come as refugees from another country.

foreign national—a person who is not a citizen or legal permanent resident of the country in which he or she currently resides.

port of entry—any place where a person may legally enter the country, including official border crossings and international airports.

refugee—a person outside of his or her country of origin who is unable or unwilling to return because of persecution or a well-founded fear of persecution on account of race, religion, nationality, membership in a particular social group, or political opinion.

terrorism—the use of violence or the threat of violence (especially against civilians) in order to achieve a political goal.

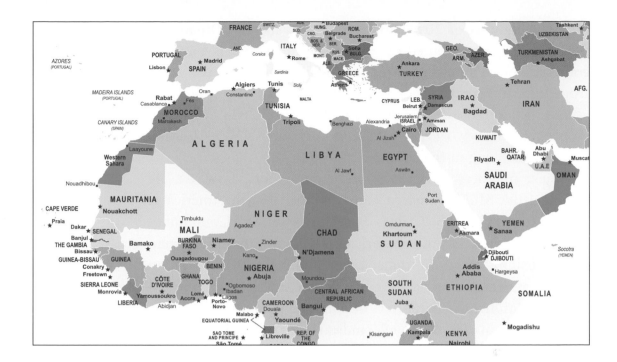

The Middle Eastern countries discussed in this book are shown in color on this map. Although definitions of what constitutes the Middle East differ, this book will include information about the major Arab states of the Arabian Peninsula and North Africa, as well as Israel, Turkey, and Iran.

immigrate to the United States. Similarly, a reformed immigration policy in Canada, instituted in 1967, enabled more people from underrepresented ethnic groups to live in that country.

The 1965 U.S. law not only brought more Middle Eastern immigrants to the United States, it invited a more diverse mix. In an essay she contributed to *Arabs in America: Building a New Future*," Helen Hatab Samhan, executive director of the Arab American Institute Foundation, notes:

> In the past 30 years, not only did new Arab immigration diversify and expand the Arab American community, it also brought about political, cultural, and religious identities that contrasted with the assimilated identity of the U.S.-born co-ethnics. Where offspring of the first (mostly Christian) immigrants had faced the intensive civic assimilation of that largely European wave, the post–World War II immigrants arrived in a wave predominantly from the Third World, a factor that would also characterize their identity and attitudes toward assimilation in general and classification in particular.

The number of Middle Eastern immigrants to the United States has swelled from fewer than 200,000 in 1970 to more than a million as of 2013. Some countries, such as Oman and Bahrain, have contributed only a few hundred to this total; by contrast, more than a quarter million immigrants have come from Iran. In Canada, Iran is the leading source of immigrants among Middle Eastern countries. Canada's 2011 National Household Survey (NHS) found more than 120,000 Iranian immigrants living in the country.

These numbers reflect only new immigrants, however. By heritage, the Middle Eastern community in North America is much larger. The U.S. Census Bureau's American Community Survey estimated the Arab American population (both Christian and Muslim) at more than 1.8 million in 2013. Iranian Americans, Israeli Americans, and Turkish Americans accounted for an additional three-quarters of a million people. Official statistics from Canada, meanwhile, indicate that in 2011 there were more than 380,000 Arab Canadians, more than 163,000 Iranian Canadians, and about 15,000 Israeli Canadians.

They're Still Coming to America

The reasons Middle Easterners leave their homelands, and how they fare once they arrive in North America, will be explored in later chapters. Although poverty does exist among Middle Eastern immigrants, generally speaking, they are better educated, earn more money, and become American citizens in higher percentages than immigrants from many other parts of the world. That's not to say that Middle Eastern immigrants do not have barriers and obstacles to overcome; in that, they are similar to other newcomers.

The motivating factors that brought Middle Easterners to North America continued for many years after immigration quotas were lifted in the 1960s. Then, beginning on September 11, 2001, the course of Middle Eastern immigration became unclear. On that day, terrorist hijackers crashed airplanes into both towers of New York's World Trade Center and into the Pentagon, outside Washington, D.C.; another plane, believed to be headed for the White House or U.S. Capitol, crashed in a field in west-

Pedestrians walk past a makeshift memorial at the Inland Regional Center (IRC) in San Bernardino, California. A mass shooting by two Muslim immigrants in December 2015 caused some American leaders to raise concerns about immigration from the Middle East.

ern Pennsylvania. In all, about 3,000 people were killed in the attacks.

The 19 terrorists were associates of al-Qaeda, the Islamic militant organization led by Osama bin Laden. Bin Laden's desire to overthrow governments he considered to be "non-Islamic" and to rid Muslim countries of non-Muslims was well known, but never before had such an attack been launched on American soil.

The hijackers were all from Middle Eastern countries, primarily Saudi Arabia. They had entered the United States legally on temporary visas as students, tourists, or businessmen, and at the time of the attack, 16 of the 19 were still in the country legally. When this fact later emerged, it stirred much debate about the U.S. immigration system.

Ultimately, the country's immigration system was revamped in an effort to address the threat of terrorism. In October 2001

President George W. Bush, flanked by members of Congress, signs the Enhanced Border Security and Visa Entry Reform Act, May 14, 2002. The legislation, passed in response to the September 11, 2001, terrorist attacks on the United States, tightened rules on the granting of visas.

Congress passed, and President George W. Bush signed, the USA Patriot Act. Among its many other provisions, the Patriot Act bolstered border enforcement (particularly along the Canadian border) and authorized the detention of foreign nationals for up to a week, during which time the government could decide whether to charge the detainee with a criminal offense or immigration violation. In 2002 the Homeland Security Act dissolved the Immigration and Naturalization Service (INS)—the federal agency, operating under the Department of Justice, that had been responsible for processing visa and naturalization applications, border control, and the apprehension of undocumented immigrants. The major responsibilities of the INS were spread among three new agencies within the newly created Department of Homeland Security. U.S. Citizenship and Immigration Services (USCIS) handles visas, naturalization applications, and the like. Customs and Border Protection (CBP) oversees the movement of people and goods across the nation's borders and at all ports of entry, and it apprehends persons trying to enter the United States illegally. Immigration and Customs Enforcement (ICE) is responsible for enforcing immigration laws and customs regulations in the interior of the country; its duties include the detention and removal of undocumented immigrants.

In addition to these and other domestic measures, the administration of President George W. Bush also pursued an aggressive foreign policy in the name of combating terrorism. Most controversially, the administration pushed for an invasion of Iraq. That invasion, which commenced in March 2003, toppled the brutal regime of Iraqi dictator Saddam Hussein. But it also plunged Iraq into chaos and, according to experts, helped destabilize the broader Middle East.

More than a dozen years after the U.S. invasion, Iraq continued to be plagued by violence and disorder. According to a United Nations report released in January 2016, at least 18,800 Iraqi civilians were killed between January 2014 and October 2015 (and the actual death toll, the UN report noted, might be substantially higher). Meanwhile, large swaths of Iraqi territory were controlled by the Islamic State, popularly known by the acronym ISIS (or, in some quarters, ISIL). The group, notorious for its barbarity, also held significant parts of Syria, which was in the midst of a bloody civil war. ISIS was one of a handful of factions fighting against the government of dictator Bashar al-Assad in the Syrian civil war. But its goals weren't limited to ousting Assad. ISIS sought to expand, through conquest, its self-styled caliphate (Islamic state).

ISIS claimed that Muslims worldwide had a duty to join the caliphate. It also called on Muslims living in countries that opposed ISIS militarily—including various Western European nations, a handful of Arab countries, the United States, Canada, and Russia—to carry out terrorist attacks in their home countries.

On November 13, 2015, nine terrorists with links to ISIS mounted a series of coordinated attacks in and around Paris, France. They murdered 130 civilians and wounded several hundred others. Seven of the terrorists were identified. All were French or Belgian citizens, and all were believed to have traveled to Syria, where they presumably fought for or received training from ISIS. One of the two unidentified terrorists was carrying a forged Syrian passport; he and the other unidentified terrorist had entered and traveled through Europe among Syrian refugees.

In the United States, the massacre in Paris quickly became part of an already contentious debate. The Syrian civil war had produced a flood of refugees—more than 4 million between early 2011 and mid-2015, according to the UN. Most of these refugees had fled to countries bordering Syria, including Turkey, Lebanon, and Jordan. But hundreds of thousands had made their way to Europe, with approximately 80,000 granted asylum in European Union (EU) countries in 2015 alone. The United States, by contrast, had accepted fewer than 2,200 Syrian refugees from 2012 to 2015. In September 2015, however, President Barack Obama pledged that the United States would welcome at least 10,000 Syrian refugees in the coming year. The president's critics immediately objected, claiming U.S. immigration authorities lacked the capacity to adequately vet that many people from a war zone. ISIS fighters, they said, could slip into the country by posing as refugees.

That argument gained traction after the Paris terrorist attacks, as at least one of the killers apparently had gotten into Europe by pretending to be a Syrian refugee. But Obama administration officials and refugee advocates pointed out that, in the matter of Syrian refugees, Europe and the United States were in vastly different positions. Refugees streamed to Europe via multiple routes. Many were guided overland through Turkey by smugglers, then made a brief boat trip to one of the small Greek islands in the Aegean Sea. With thousands arriving on those islands every day, Greek authorities were overwhelmed. They often granted Syrians permission to continue into mainland Europe after taking fingerprints and asking a few cursory questions. By contrast, being accepted into the United States as a refugee involves multiple screenings, including law enforcement and intelligence database searches as well as a face-to-face interview. The process takes 18 to 24 months. Pretending to be a refugee, the Obama administration argued, would be perhaps the single most difficult way for an ISIS recruit to get into the United States.

Nonetheless, in the wake of the Paris attacks, 31 governors said they opposed allowing any Syrian refugees into their state. Most of the candidates for the Republican Party's 2016 presidential nomination also declared their support for a full ban on Syrian refugees entering the United States, although two of the candidates—Senator Ted Cruz of Texas, and Jeb Bush, the former governor of Florida—said Syrian refugees who were Christian should be eligible for admission, but those who were Muslim should not. "There is no meaningful risk of Christians committing acts of terror," Cruz asserted.

On December 2, three weeks after the Paris terrorist attacks, two shooters killed 14 people and wounded more than 20 others at a community center in San Bernardino, California. The shooters—an American named Syed Farook and his Pakistani-born wife, Tashfeen Malik—were Muslim. While their motives weren't clear (and both died in a shoot-out with police), Malik

 A New Country, A New Life

Najat Mounir's outlook has been shaped by what she describes as "the unusual aspect of the path my life took, and all the extraordinary events that took place during the journey." Mounir's journey began in Casablanca, where she was the 5th of 10 children born to a poor Moroccan couple. At 16, she was wed to an illiterate man three times her age—an arranged marriage that lasted about a year. Mounir went to college in France but soon became pregnant and dropped out of school.

Back in Morocco, she took a job at an airport, but she began dreaming of a fresh start in the United States. She eventually immigrated, settling first in New York City, then in Las Vegas, and finally in a small town in Washington. Mounir's dream has not always been easy. She endured a long separation from her son, who continued to live in Morocco; she's gone through bankruptcy; and she raised a second son as a single mother. But she has also experienced a great deal of joy in her adopted country.

In her essay "Awareness! What Does It Take?" Mounir writes, "I shared joy, pain, and dreams with people of all nations here in America, and found out, we are all the same. Here I am treated as a human being in my community. . . . I am not a case file, a statistic, or a number. I am not looked upon as a stranger, a foreigner, or a terrorist either. Instead of the image of a stranger Arab Muslim woman, people here know me as the Arab Muslim woman who is Zacharia's mom."

Arab Americans enjoy a summer festival in New York City.

had pledged allegiance to the leader of ISIS in a social-media post right before the rampage began.

That fact alone led some Americans to clamor for the government to take drastic action. Donald Trump, the front-runner for the Republican Party's presidential nomination, called not simply for restricting the entry of Syrian refugees but for the "total and complete shutdown of Muslims entering the United States until our country's representatives can figure out what is going on."

According to a Washington Post/ABC News poll, 60 percent of Americans rejected Trump's suggestion. But a significant minority—36 percent—agreed that a ban on Muslim immigrants and travelers entering the United States was warranted. Since the terrorist attacks of 2001, some Americans have come to regard Muslims—especially those of Middle Eastern heritage—with suspicion.

 # Text-Dependent Questions

1. Which country is the leading source of Middle Eastern immigrants to Canada?
2. What happened on September 11, 2001?
3. Why did 31 U.S. governors call for a ban on Syrian refugees entering the United States?

 # Research Project

Select one Middle Eastern country, and read about its history. Then construct a timeline that includes major events.

2 FRIENDS, ENEMIES, AND NEIGHBORS

To understand the modern Middle East, and to get a sense of why people from the region emigrate, a little historical background is helpful. The Middle East is considered a cradle of civilization. Agriculture developed in Mesopotamia, the region between the Tigris and Euphrates Rivers in present-day Iraq, around 8000 BCE. By the fourth millennium BCE the world's first cities had sprung up in southern Mesopotamia under the Sumerians; the Sumerians also created the earliest-known system of writing.

Over the centuries the Middle East gave rise to a number of important kingdoms and empires, including ancient Egypt, Babylonia, and Assyria. Located at a strategically important crossroads between the Mediterranean world and the Far East, the region also attracted many foreign conquerors, including Alexander the Great in the fourth century BCE.

The Roman Empire at its height controlled much of the Middle East, including Asia Minor (modern-day Turkey), Mesopotamia, the eastern shores of the Mediterranean (territory that today includes Syria, Lebanon, and Israel), Egypt, and a long swath of land running along the coast of North Africa from Egypt to present-day Morocco. As far as the Middle East is con-

◀ Constructed in the mid-14th century CE, the Sultan Hassan Mosque in Cairo, Egypt, is an outstanding example of Islamic architecture. Islam dominates the contemporary Middle East and North Africa, where more than 9 in 10 people are Muslims.

cerned, however, Rome's most enduring legacy may be its treatment of one of the peoples under its dominion: the Jews.

A people unified by their monotheistic religion—and specifically by the belief that God had established a covenant with them as His chosen people—the Jews had established a powerful kingdom, with its spiritual and political capital at Jerusalem, by around the 11th century BCE. Over the ensuing centuries, parts or all of the Jewish land fell to a succession of conquerors, including the Assyrians, the Babylonians, and the Macedonians under Alexander the Great.

In 63 BCE Rome took control of Judea, as the Jews' land was called. But the Romans permitted the Jews a degree of autonomy. However, the Romans clamped down hard on a Jewish revolt that began in CE 66. In 70, after four years of fighting, the Romans sacked Jerusalem and destroyed the Jews' Holy Temple. After suppressing another revolt, the Bar Kochba Rebellion, in 165, the Romans forbade Jews to enter Jerusalem, exiled the majority of the Jewish population, and renamed the area Palestine (after the Jews' traditional enemies, the Philistines).

By this time another major monotheistic faith, Christianity, had sprung up in the region. That religion centered on Jesus of Nazareth, a Jew whom the Romans executed around CE 30. Followers came to believe that Jesus was the Son of God and that his death redeemed sinful humanity. The Romans initially persecuted Christians, but in the early fourth century the Roman emperor Constantine converted to the new faith, and by the end

 Words to Understand in This Chapter

covenant—a formal, solemn, and binding agreement.

mandate—authority to carry out a policy; an order or commission granted by the League of Nations to a member nation for the establishment of a responsible government over a former colony or other conquered territory after World War I.

monotheistic—believing in one God.

This ancient tilework shows Assyrian soldiers preparing for a battle. Mesopotamia, as the land between the Tigris and Euphrates Rivers was known, was home to some of the earliest human civilizations.

of the century Christianity had become the empire's official state religion. This greatly facilitated Christianity's spread.

The Rise of Islam

Beginning in the seventh century, the Middle East came under the influence of the third major monotheistic religion to arise in the region: Islam. The faithful believe that around 610 Muhammad, an Arab merchant living in Mecca (in present-day Saudi Arabia), received the first of a lifelong series of revelations from Allah (God). Soon thereafter Muhammad began preaching Allah's message—the essence of which is that there is only one God and that believers must submit to God's will. Forced to leave Mecca in 622, Muhammad and his followers settled in Medina. For the remainder of the decade, the Muslims (as adher-

ents of Islam are called) fought the pagan Meccans, eventually triumphing and converting their enemies to the Islamic faith.

Soon after Muhammad's death in 632, a formidable Arab army emerged from the Arabian Peninsula and began a remarkable series of conquests that, in a matter of decades, would spread Islam's influence across the Middle East and North Africa and, by the early part of the eighth century, into Spain.

Yet the Islamic world was never completely united. Over the years, rival dynasties struggled for political control as various Islamic empires rose and fell. And religious differences among the faithful also emerged. A major doctrinal rift, which dates to Islam's earliest days, stemmed from the question of who should succeed Muhammad as caliph, or leader of Islam. One group, which came to be called the Sunni, believed that the caliph should be elected from among the Prophet's followers. Another

European Christian knights under Godfrey of Bouillon celebrate the taking of Jerusalem from the Muslims during the First Crusade, July 15, 1099. Possession of the city of Jerusalem—holy ground for all three of the major monotheistic religions that originated in the Middle East—has been a source of conflict for centuries.

group, known as the Shia, insisted that only a blood relative of Muhammad could serve as caliph. The split became quite bitter. Today, most Muslims worldwide follow the Sunni branch of Islam, though in a few Middle Eastern countries—notably Iran and Iraq—Shiites constitute a majority.

If Islam has suffered its share of internal conflicts, over the centuries relations among Muslims, Christians, and Jews have also frequently been troubled. This is the case despite the fact that the three faiths share many important connections. Christianity, of course, developed from Judaism; the two faiths diverged with the figure of Jesus, whom Christians believe to be the Messiah that God promised the Jewish people. But Islam, too, shares much with the Jewish tradition. Like Jews, Muslims trace their ancestry to the patriarch Abraham. Islam's prophets include Abraham, as well as Moses and Jesus. And for adherents of all three religions, the city of Jerusalem has special religious significance: for Jews, it is the site where the Holy Temple once stood; for Christians, it's where Jesus taught and was crucified; for Muslims, it's where the prophet Muhammad ascended to heaven. Much blood has been shed over control of Jerusalem, from the Crusades of the Middle Ages, during which European Christian knights fought to drive out the Muslims (and also massacred many Jews), to the present-day Palestinian-Israeli conflict.

The Ottoman Era

During the 16th century, the powerful Ottoman Empire began to extend its influence throughout the Middle East and North Africa. Though Muslims, the Ottomans—who also conquered southeastern Europe and the strategic area between the Black and Caspian Seas—were ethnic Turks rather than Arabs.

From their capital of Istanbul, in modern-day Turkey, the Ottomans administered their large empire through local governors. They were fairly liberal, allowing freedom of religion and limited self-rule among conquered peoples. Nevertheless, many Arabs deeply resented the idea of being under the authority of the Ottoman sultan, not to mention the taxes they were com-

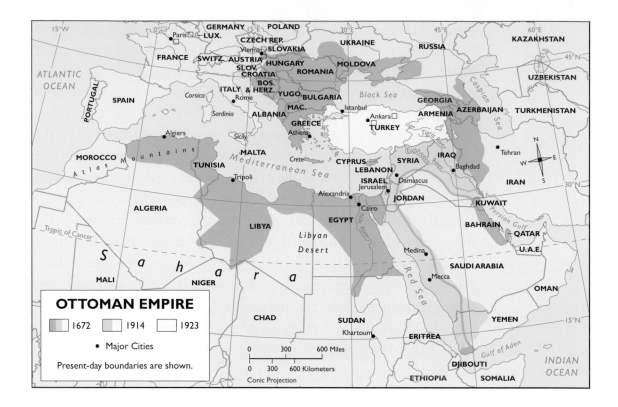

OTTOMAN EMPIRE

	1672		1914		1923

• Major Cities

Present-day boundaries are shown.

0   300   600 Miles

0   300   600 Kilometers

Conic Projection

pelled to pay to the empire.

In the opinion of most historians, the Ottoman Empire reached its peak during the reign of Süleyman the Magnificent (1520–1566). Over the next 350 years, corruption would weaken the empire from within, while the rise of European powers such as Russia, France, and Great Britain would pressure it from without. By 1914 the Ottoman Empire still held Mesopotamia, Palestine, and the Hejaz (the western part of present-day Saudi Arabia), but European colonial powers controlled, through various arrangements, much of North Africa, including Algeria, Morocco, and Tunisia (France); Egypt and the Sudan (Britain); and Libya (Italy).

By the outbreak of World War I in 1914, European powers had whittled away much of the Ottoman Empire. After the war, League of Nations mandates gave administrative control of the remainder (except Turkey) to Great Britain and France.

World War I and Its Aftermath

When World War I broke out in 1914, the Ottoman Empire aligned itself with Germany and Austria-Hungary against the Allies—principally Great Britain, France, and Russia. (The

United States entered the war on the side of the Allies three years later.)

Following a disastrous campaign on Turkey's Gallipoli Peninsula in 1915, the British attempted to strike a blow against the Ottoman Turks by fomenting an Arab rebellion against them. In return for his support, the British promised the leader of that rebellion, Sharif Hussein bin Ali, that an Arab state would be created from Ottoman territory after the war. The exact boundaries of that state were never specified.

In 1917 the British also attempted to shore up Jewish support for the war effort by promising to "view with favour the establishment in Palestine of a national home for the Jewish people." Although the document in which this promise was made, the Balfour Declaration, explicitly stated that "nothing shall be done which may prejudice the civil and religious rights of existing non-Jewish communities in Palestine," Jews and Arabs would prove unable to share the land peacefully.

In the meantime, however, the British had concluded a secret agreement with the French regarding the shape of the postwar Middle East. By the terms of the 1916 Sykes-Picot accord, the two countries agreed to divide the Ottoman territories of the

Istanbul was the seat of Ottoman power from the mid-15th to the early 20th century. Today the Turkish city is a popular tourist destination, offering such attractions as the Blue Mosque.

region between themselves. The specifics of the agreement would be rendered obsolete by events on the ground, as Britain succeeded in conquering Palestine and Mesopotamia.

After the end of World War I in 1918, the defeated Ottoman Turks were forced to give up the remnants of their Middle Eastern empire (the modern Republic of Turkey emerged in 1923). The newly created League of Nations granted Great Britain and France mandates to administer Arab territories formerly under the control of the Ottoman Turks. Britain received the mandate for Mesopotamia (Iraq) and Palestine (which it later divided into Palestine and the Transjordan); France was awarded the mandate for Syria (including Lebanon) and the Hejaz.

 Birthplace of Religions

The Middle East has given birth to the world's three most important monotheistic religions: Judaism, Christianity, and Islam.

Today, more than 90 percent of Middle Easterners and North Africans are followers of Islam. Yet none of the four largest Muslim nations (Indonesia, Pakistan, India, and Bangladesh) are located in the Middle East. Like other religions, Islam can be interpreted in different ways. Nonetheless, there are five basic beliefs, or pillars, that define the religion: faith, specifically that there is only one God and that Muhammad was his last and greatest prophet; prayers, said five times daily; charity to provide for the needy; fasting; and pilgrimage to the holy city of Mecca. Most Middle Eastern Muslims are either Sunni or Shiite, two branches of Islam that developed over the question of who was Muhammad's rightful successor. In the Middle East, most Shiites live in Iran, Iraq, or southern Lebanon.

Middle Eastern Christians are relatively few in number and, in some cases, persecuted or limited in their ability to practice their faith. They believe in a three-person God, or Holy Trinity (Father, Son, and Holy Spirit), and believe that the Son, Jesus, was crucified and resurrected, in the process redeeming humanity. Most Middle Eastern Christians are members of Eastern Rite churches (Armenian, Chaldean, Coptic, Maronite, Melkite, and Syrian), which are affiliated with the Roman Catholic Church. However, Eastern Rite churches are semi-autonomous, meaning they observe the core beliefs of the Catholic Church as well as their own customs and rites. For example, Eastern Rite clergy are permitted to marry, while Roman Catholic priests are not.

Not all Eastern Rite churches share the same beliefs or operate in the same region. For instance, the Maronites, unlike other Christians, believe that Jesus Christ was fully divine, and not also human. Most

The seeds of several intractable problems were sown during the post–World War I era. For example, the Kurds, a non-Arab people who occupy mountainous regions in modern-day Turkey, Iraq, Iran, and Syria, were supposed to be given a homeland, according to the terms of the Treaty of Sèvres. That did not happen, and Kurdish nationalism, particularly in Turkey, has led to bloodshed and remains a concern of the Turkish government. The kingdom of Iraq, which achieved independence in 1932 under a British-installed monarch born in Mecca, incorporated three distinct groups with separate national interests: ethnic Kurds, Sunni Muslims, and Shia Muslims. In the aftermath of the 2003 war that ousted Iraq's longtime dictator, Saddam Hussein, horrific violence played out between Iraq's Sunni and

Maronites live in Lebanon, composing about one-fourth of the country's population. While there are more than 4 million Coptic Christians living in Egypt, they are discriminated against and often severely persecuted. Iraq used to be home to a significant Chaldean Christian community, accounting for about 3 percent of the country's population. Today, however, Chaldean Christians--who still speak Aramaic, the language Jesus is believed to have spoken--make up less than 1 percent of Iraq's population. Large numbers of Chaldean Christians fled Iraq in the violent aftermath of the 2003 U.S.-led invasion. Pockets of Christian communities can also be found in Jordan, Israel, and Iran, but Christianity is against the law in Saudi Arabia.

More than 8 million people live in Israel, and about 6 million of them are Jews. According to Jewish teaching, Jews are God's chosen people and are awaiting a Messiah, a deliverer. In 1948, following World War II, the State of Israel was established. Among the many Jews who immigrated to Israel during that period were Jewish survivors of the Holocaust in Europe and Jews living in Arab countries.

The Druze, members of a secretive sect that originated about a thousand years ago as an offshoot of Islam, believe their religion to be a reinterpretation of Islam, Christianity, and Judaism. But they do not observe religious rituals or accept converts; they do believe in reincarnation. Most of the estimated 1 million Druze today live in Syria, Lebanon, or Israel. In Israel, the Druze have their own legal and educational systems.

Shia communities. And in Palestine, Zionism—the movement to create a Jewish state—sparked violence between Jewish settlers and Palestinian Arabs. In the early years of the 21st century, the Jewish-Palestinian conflict remains at the heart of Middle East violence and instability.

Post-World War II Developments

During the period between World War II (1939–1945) and the 1960s, nation after nation in the Middle East and North Africa gained independence. In many cases, peace and stability have proved more elusive. Israel, for example, fought wars against its Arab neighbors at its founding in 1948, in 1967, and again in 1973; terrorism against Israel, particularly by Palestinians who want to establish their own homeland, has occurred continually since the 1960s. Iraq invaded its neighbors Iran in 1980 and Kuwait in 1990. The former invasion led to an extremely costly

Thousands of Egyptians gather in Cairo's Tahrir Square to protest against the government, February 2011. The Arab Spring demonstrations eventually drove longtime ruler Hosni Mubarak to resign.

eight-year stalemate; the latter, to defeat at the hands of a U.S.-led coalition in 1991. Lebanon suffered through a civil war that lasted from 1975 to 1990 and claimed more than 140,000 lives. Sudan's civil war was even more pitiless, leading to an estimated 2 million deaths between 1983 and 2011, when South Sudan gained independence from Sudan. Algeria has seen long-running violence between Arabs and Berbers, and between those who support fundamentalist Islamic rule and those who favor a moderate, secular government.

Syria's civil war, which erupted in 2011, had claimed more than 200,000 lives by January 2016. In tiny Yemen, the death toll from a civil war that began in 2015 had reached 6,000 by early 2016. The conflict, in the view of Mideast analysts, was fueled by the bitter rivalry between two regional powers: Saudi Arabia and Iran.

In the political realm, the Middle East is remarkable for its dearth of fully democratic, representative governments. Notable exceptions include Israel and Turkey, along with Tunisia.

For a while, it appeared that events in Tunisia had unleashed a tide of democratization throughout the region, which

Destroyed tanks outside of a ruined mosque in Azaz, Syria. The civil war that began in 2011 threatens to destabilize much of the Middle East.

These Syrian refugees are housed in a camp near the border in Turkey. Conflicts in Syria, Iraq, and Afghanistan have created a refugee crisis, as millions of people flee from the fighting.

observers dubbed the Arab Spring. In December 2010, protests broke out against the repressive regime of Tunisian strongman Zine El Abidine Ben Ali, who'd been the country's president since seizing power in 1987. By January 2011, Ben Ali had been forced to flee the country. Across the Arab world—from Egypt, the most populous Arab state, to the tiny island nation of Bahrain—citizens followed the example of the Tunisians. They demanded political reform and greater personal freedoms in their countries.

In a few places, such as Jordan and Morocco, leaders enacted modest reforms in response to the Arab Spring. But other regimes violently suppressed the protests. In Syria, Bashar al-Assad's brutal crackdown triggered that country's civil war.

In Egypt and Libya, pro-democracy forces appeared to have won significant victories. The gains, however, proved fleeting. A revolution in Egypt ousted dictator Hosni Mubarak in February

2011. The following year, parliamentary elections were held, with conservative Islamist parties, including the Muslim Brotherhood, winning the lion's share of seats. Muslim Brotherhood candidate Mohammed Morsi narrowly won Egypt's 2011 presidential election. But Morsi and his Islamist allies marginalized liberal and nonreligious groups. They pushed through a new constitution that restricted freedom of speech and bolstered the role of Islam in Egypt. Morsi declared that Egyptian courts had no right to challenge his orders. In July 2013, amid growing unrest, the Egyptian army ousted Morsi in a coup. The Muslim Brotherhood was ultimately outlawed. Since then, Egypt has faced terrorist attacks from radical Islamic groups.

In February 2011, Libyans rose up against Muammar Gaddafi, who'd ruled his North African nation with an iron fist since 1969. With military aid from foreign countries, including the United States, the Libyan revolutionaries overthrew Gaddafi in October 2011. But chaos ensued, as local militias and groups affiliated with the terrorist organizations al-Qaeda and ISIS battled one another for power.

Except in Tunisia, which appears to have developed into a stable democracy, the promise of the Arab Spring wasn't fully realized. The Middle East continues to be roiled by unrest and dominated by regimes that restrict the rights of their citizens. Given those circumstances, it's not surprising that many people seek to emigrate.

Text-Dependent Questions

1. Identify the three major monotheistic religions that arose in the Middle East.
2. When was the Balfour Declaration made? What did it promise?
3. What was the Arab Spring?

Research Project

Use a library or the Internet to find out more about the Ottoman Empire. Write a two-page report on the empire's rise and fall.

3 COMING TO AMERICA

People from the Middle East have been immigrating to North America for more than a century. Not surprisingly, they've been motivated by a variety of factors, some of which have assumed greater importance at different times. In addition, North Americans' attitudes toward newcomers have varied.

Push and Pull Factors for Middle Eastern Immigrants

Middle Easterners have been coming to the United States since the late 1800s. Over time, particularly since the second half of the 20th century, economics has been less of a motivating factor for emigration, as education, politics, and the desire for certain freedoms (especially religious freedoms) have taken greater precedence. And while many of the early immigrants were Christians, the number of Muslims coming to North America from the Middle East has increased significantly in the past few decades.

The first wave of Middle Eastern immigrants came from modern-day Lebanon, Syria, Jordan, and Israel (including Palestinians). They emigrated primarily for economic opportu-

◀ The Registry Hall on Ellis Island, circa 1905. Between 1892 and 1954, about 12 million immigrants to the United States passed through this famous immigration station in New York Harbor.

nities and to escape religious persecution. In sociological terms, they were motivated to come to North America because of both "push" and "pull" factors. Push factors are problems within the homeland, such as civil war, religious or political persecution, poverty, and famine. Pull factors attract people to a country: civil liberties, employment and educational opportunities, the desire to be with family, and so on. When both push and pull factors are weak, there's little incentive for migration. For example, relatively few people immigrate to North America from wealthy and stable Qatar or the United Arab Emirates.

What were some of the push and pull factors for early Middle Eastern immigrants? According to Michael W. Suleiman, editor of *Arabs in America: Building a New Future*, the Greater Syrian economy was hit hard in the mid-1800s with the emergence of Japan as competition in the silk industry, and again at the end of the century, when a blight took its toll on vineyards. During the late 1800s, Christians faced oppression from the Ottoman regime, which pitted them against Muslims. While not well off, Arab Muslims had a higher social status than Christians. "The threat of losing that 'high' status made many Muslims susceptible to suggestions from local Ottoman rulers that their Christian neighbors were the cause of rather than companions in their troubles," notes Suleiman. "The worsened social

 Words to Understand in This Chapter

annexation—the act of formally incorporating new territory into a larger political unit or state.

Diaspora—the community of Jews living outside Palestine.

emigration—the act of leaving one country to settle in another.

pull factors—positive characteristics of, or situations in, a particular country (for example, civil liberties, employment or educational opportunities, the presence of family members) that attract prospective immigrants to that country.

push factors—negative characteristics of, or situations in, a country (for example, civil war, religious or political persecution, poverty, famine) that make people want to leave that country.

Interior of a Coptic Christian church in Cairo, Egypt. Christian minorities in the Muslim countries of the Middle East have often faced persecution. This has led some Arab Christians to leave for the United States or Canada, where they can be free to practice their religion.

and economic conditions in Syria in the mid-1800s and the beginning of the disintegration of feudalism, especially among the Druze, produced social turmoil that erupted in sectarian riots in which thousands of Christians perished." Many Maronite Christians, in particular, chose to flee to the United States for what they thought would be a temporary stay.

For the most part, these early immigrants didn't want to establish deep roots in America; they earned money by peddling, working in restaurants, and doing crochet and lace work. But after World War I, Suleiman explains, that attitude changed. "It became clear to large numbers of Arabs in North America that it was not possible to go 'home' again and that the United States and Canada were their homes."

More recently, two pull factors, education and reuniting with family members, have motivated much immigration to North America from various Arab countries. For other immigrants,

however, jobs are the primary motivator to come to North America. For example, an estimated 90 percent of Yemeni immigrants to the United States are unaccompanied men who want to work and save money to support their families back in Yemen.

A spike in Middle Eastern immigration to the United States followed the 1991 Gulf War. In the 1980s, according to U.S. immigration data, 19,533 Iraqis had immigrated to the United States; during the 1990s, that number more than doubled, to 40,749. In the wake of the Gulf War, Kurds in northern Iraq and Shia Muslims in the southern part of the country rose up in an attempt to overthrow the regime of Saddam Hussein. The uprisings were brutally suppressed, and hundreds of thousands of Iraqis the regime suspected of disloyalty were arrested, tortured, and, in many cases, murdered. Even those whose safety was not immediately threatened had reason to want to leave Iraq. Because of the regime's failure to comply with disarmament provisions

The 1991 Gulf War, plus subsequent Kurdish and Shiite uprisings and years of crippling economic sanctions, combined to produce a spike in Iraqi immigration to North America in the 1990s.

contained in the Gulf War cease-fire agreement, the international community imposed economic sanctions on Iraq. Those sanctions further devastated the country's economy and impoverished millions of Iraqis during the 1990s.

But the effects of the war and its aftermath weren't confined to Iraqis. Palestinians, for example, suffered considerable economic harm. Their troubles began with the events that led to the Gulf War—Iraq's August 1990 invasion and annexation of Kuwait, its southern neighbor. The UN quickly passed resolutions condemning Iraq's actions, declaring the annexation of Kuwait invalid, and demanding an immediate withdrawal of all Iraqi troops from Kuwait.

The Arab League—whose members include both Iraq and Kuwait—soon met in emergency session in Cairo, Egypt. A majority of the Arab League's 21 members endorsed the UN resolutions. But Palestine, which was represented by the Palestine Liberation Organization (PLO)—the group that had taken the lead in the quest to secure a Palestinian state in Israeli-occupied

Israeli soldiers examine a Palestinian's vehicle at a roadblock in the West Bank. The conflict between Israel and the Palestinians has contributed to a large exodus of Palestinian Christians from the occupied territories.

territory—voted against the Arab League majority. Over the years, the PLO received significant financial backing from Iraq and Kuwait. Iraq, however, had the region's largest army—and it had taken part in every Arab-Israeli war since 1948. Kuwait's armed forces, by contrast, were insubstantial. PLO leader Yasser Arafat gambled that Palestinian interests would be better served by maintaining good relations with Saddam Hussein than by opposing Iraq's annexation of Kuwait.

Events would prove Arafat wrong. After the Gulf War, which saw Iraqi forces soundly defeated and Kuwait liberated by a U.S.-led international coalition, Kuwait cut off its funding to the PLO. It also retaliated against ordinary Palestinians. Kuwait expelled approximately 400,000 Palestinian guest workers, many of whom held high-paying jobs in the country's oil industry. Other oil-rich Arab states in the Persian Gulf region followed suit. Meanwhile, most Palestinians (and Yemenis) who'd been working in Iraq before the war lost their jobs.

Job prospects in the West Bank and Gaza Strip, particularly for the most educated of the expelled Palestinians, were dismal. "This meant their only other option for survival was the U.S.," notes sociologist Louise A. Cainkar, who has studied Arab immigration to the United States.

Even as many Palestinians formerly employed in the Persian Gulf states sought to relocate to North America, a glimmer of hope for a Palestinian homeland emerged. In 1993 Israel and the PLO signed the first of a series of agreements known as the Oslo Accords. The PLO officially recognized Israel and renounced violence against the Jewish state. In return, Israel recognized the PLO as the legitimate representative of the Palestinian people, and Palestinians were granted limited self-government in parts of the West Bank and Gaza Strip under an interim administrative body known as the Palestinian Authority, or PA. The PA would be headed by Yasser Arafat.

The Oslo Accords were notably short on specifics. It was hoped that as the two sides gained trust in each other, Israeli troops could gradually be withdrawn from the West Bank and

Refuge for a Refugee

Mamoon Jarrah's name aptly sums up his life story: In Arabic, Mamoon means "take refuge"; Jarrah translates to "the surgeon."

Jarrah was only two years old when he and his family were forced to leave Akkar, Palestine (now Akko, Israel), as a result of the 1948 Israeli-Arab war. They lived in Lebanon for two years before moving to Syria. "His father was an educated man, a mechanical engineer, but as refugees, the family lost everything," says Samar Jarrah, his wife. "As a child, Mamoon realized he was different from his wealthy Syrian classmates because they did not go to the relief agency for rations." He was intelligent, athletic, and popular, but Jarrah's refugee status held him back; because he did not have a passport, for instance, he could not travel to other countries for sports competitions.

Jarrah went to college and then to medical school in Syria, earning his M.D. and completing a residency in anesthesiology. When a medical school professor expressed his belief that the American medical system was superior to the European system, Jarrah and several classmates decided they wanted to study in the United States. They hired a tutor to teach them English, learning enough of the language to take the medical school entrance exams. Jarrah passed the exams and came to the United States on a student visa in 1973. At first, the young doctor struggled a bit: his English was limited, he had a new culture to get used to, and, as a student, he found that money was often tight. But he completed an internship, a surgical residency, and a fellowship program in peripheral vascular surgery in New Jersey. Jarrah then received fellowship training in cardiovascular surgery in South Carolina and completed a residency in cardiovascular and thoracic surgery in Mississippi.

Jarrah originally intended to return to Syria. His father had passed away soon after he came to the United States, and as the eldest son, he felt responsible for his family. (Eventually, his mother and two of his brothers also came to the United States.) However, as a Palestinian refugee without a passport, he would have had difficulty making a living as a physician in Syria. "He thought, 'Why say no to all the rights of being an American citizen?'" says his wife.

Jarrah, once a refugee with no rights, did become an American citizen. Since 1985 he has had a practice in vascular and thoracic surgery in Port Charlotte, Florida. "His journey to America has been emotionally draining, and there were times when he wondered if he would make it," says Samar Jarrah. "But now he has absolute freedom."

Gaza, with the PA assuming increasing responsibility for security, and that Israel and the PA would be able to negotiate acceptable compromises on a wide range of contentious matters. The Oslo process was supposed to culminate in the creation of an independent Palestinian state at peace with Israel. The exact borders of that future state, like almost every other difficult issue, would have to be negotiated.

To protect Israeli settlers, a security fence has been constructed in the West Bank that separates them from Palestinian villages.

Several extremist Palestinian groups—such as Hamas and Islamic Jihad—actively opposed the Oslo process. So did hard-line Israeli settlers, who believed it was their right and even their religious duty to inhabit all the land encompassed by the biblical Kingdom of Israel, including the West Bank.

The Oslo process soon faltered. In February 1994 an Israeli settler went on a shooting rampage in the West Bank city of Hebron, killing 29 Palestinians and wounding 125 others who were worshiping in a shrine known as the Cave of the Patriarchs. Two months later, in April, a Hamas suicide bomber killed five Israeli civilians in the city of Hadera. In 1995 an Israeli extrem-ist assassinated Yitzhak Rabin, Israel's prime minister and a champion of the Oslo Accords, at a peace rally. Hamas and Islamic Jihad launched a wave of deadly suicide bombings in 1996. That prompted Israeli security forces to crack down in the West Bank and Gaza, which in turn increased resentment among ordinary Palestinians.

In elections held in 1996, Benjamin Netanyahu, a vocal opponent of the Oslo Accords, became Israel's prime minister. The already-foundering peace process came to a grinding halt under Netanyahu's administration. While the more moderate Ehud Barak defeated Netanyahu in 1999 to become prime minister, his attempts to revive the Oslo process proved futile. Oslo's death knell, most analysts believe, came in 2000. That year, President Bill Clinton hosted Barak and Arafat at a summit in Camp David, Maryland. The leaders failed to reach agreement on acceptable borders for a Palestinian state, and the summit broke up amid bitter recriminations. Meanwhile, violence in the West Bank and Gaza intensified, in what would become a five-year-long Palestinian uprising known as the Al-Aqsa intifada.

These events forced Palestinians who'd come to the United States to study—often for advanced degrees in technical fields—to reevaluate their long-range plans. Many had intended to return home and use their expertise to help build a Palestinian

Israel's prime minister, Benjamin Netanyahu, has opposed plans to form a Palestinian state in the West Bank.

A masked Palestinian-American activist marches in a pro-Palestine rally in Washington, D.C.

state. But that option had effectively been foreclosed: there wasn't going to be a Palestinian state, at least not for the foreseeable future, and Israeli restrictions on residency and work would make it difficult simply to earn a living. As a result, many Palestinians sought to remain in the United States after they'd obtained their degrees.

In the years since the Al-Aqsa intifada, conditions for

Palestinians in the West Bank and Gaza Strip have remained grim. Israel did pull all its settlers and military forces out of Gaza in 2005, but that didn't lead to stability or prosperity. In 2007 Hamas—which was part of a Palestinian Authority unity government—broke with the PA and seized control of Gaza. Hamas-sponsored terrorist incursions and rocket attacks led to major Israeli military operations in Gaza in 2008–2009, 2012, and 2014. These, and an ongoing Israeli blockade, devastated Gaza. In the West Bank, meanwhile, new Israeli settlements continued to be built, and in 2015 Benjamin Netanyahu—who'd become prime minister again in 2009—vowed never to permit an independent Palestinian state.

Given such developments, the sociologist Louise Cainkar has noted, "one might expect Palestinian immigration to be even higher than it is. . . . But counterbalancing [these push factors] has been a Palestinian determination to stay on their land so it would not be confiscated by the Israeli government."

Push factors spurred a wave of Iraqi immigration to North America since the 2003 U.S.-led invasion of Iraq. Years of violence and chaos ensued, prompting many Iraqis to seek safety outside their homeland. The trend can be seen in U.S. immigration numbers. In 2004 about 3,500 Iraqis immigrated to the United States. By 2009 the number topped 12,000. Two years later, more than 21,000 Iraqis immigrated to the United States.

Emigration from Israel

In the 18 centuries between Rome's suppression of the Bar Kochba Rebellion in 135 and the establishment of the State of Israel in 1948, Jews settled all over the world. The Diaspora—as the totality of Jews living outside Palestine is called—included significant communities in the United States and Canada. Even today, more Jews live in the United States than in Israel.

Today migration between Israel and North America is a complex, two-way process, as Gallya Lahav and Asher Arian note in their article "Israelis in a Jewish Diaspora: The Multiple Dilemmas of a Globalized Group." Using Israeli emigration data as their source, Lahav and Arian detected several trends: "a continuing stream of Israeli immigrants to the U.S., a rise in the number of Israelis returning to Israel to live, and the emergence of a new category of 'transnationals'—individuals with footholds in both the United States and Israel."

In her book *Kibbutzniks in the Diaspora*, Naama Sabar describes some of the "push-pull factors" that contribute to Israeli emigration. "The main pull factors cited are financial prospects, better job opportunities, first-order family ties in the United States . . . and more rapid upward mobility (mainly achieved through higher education). For some, push factors include the economic and political situation in Israel, though not the security situation per se; wars which result in greater solidarity (e.g., the Six-Day War) tend to lower the tendency to emigrate."

The Jewish Israelis who come to the United States might stay temporarily or seek citizenship, but many are from the wealthier sector. "The majority of Israeli emigrants can no longer be described as marginal members of society, or 'weaklings,'" write Lahav and Arian.

Meanwhile, the escalation of violence in the West Bank and the Gaza Strip beginning in 2000 sparked the emigration of a large number of Christians from those areas. Many headed to the United States or Canada. One Palestinian Authority adviser on Christians and church affairs estimated that the number of Christians in the West Bank declined from 35,000 in 1997 to 25,000 in 2002, noted Dr. Daphne Tsimhoni in her article "Christians Fleeing Palestinian Controlled Areas." Other estimates put the number of Christians in the West Bank significantly higher—about 50,000 as of 2010—but there was broad consensus that Christians were steadily emigrating.

Changing Demographics

For many years Middle Eastern immigrants were overwhelmingly Christian. With the most recent arrivals, however, a larger percentage are adherents of Islam.

Aber Kawas, director of youth activities for the Arab-American Association of New York, speaks at a rally in Columbus Circle opposing anti-immigrant xenophobia.

Writing in the summer 2001 issue of the *Middle East Quarterly*, journalist Alexander Rose stated, "Prior to 1965 . . . only small numbers of Muslims lived in the United States; and there was little communal activity, owing mostly to their own lack of education and a worry about provoking prejudice. After 1965, however, because the immigration act of that year laid down a preference for professionals, scientists, and artists of 'exceptional ability,' the Muslim community benefited from an influx of educated, talented individuals who quickly developed financial muscle."

While the number of Middle Eastern Muslim immigrants has increased, Christians still constitute the majority of Arab Americans. According to a report released in 2009 by the Arab American National Museum, which is based in Dearborn, Michigan, 65 to 70 percent of Arab Americans are Christians. Of this group, Catholics account for the largest share, followed

AHMED S MARKET & BAKERY
313-846-6666
مطعم واسواق بغداد
313-846-9666

BREAD + PIZZA
CHICKEN WINGS

15337

BAGHDAD
313 846-6666
846-9666

FISH
YOU BUY
WE FRY

OPEN
PIZZA
ACCEPTED HERE

The signs on this Dearborn restaurant, written in both English and Arabic, reflect the diversity of the neighborhood.

by Orthodox Christians and then Protestants. Muslims, meanwhile, make up about 25 to 30 percent of the Arab American community.

In 2010, according to U.S. Census Bureau estimates, the total Arab American population stood at more than 1.96 million. That represented an increase of about 72 percent since 2000. For various reasons, however, some groups believe the Census Bureau has significantly undercounted Arab Americans. The Washington, D.C.–based Arab American Institute, for example, estimated the 2010 Arab American population at more than 3.6 million.

More Arab Americans trace their ancestry to Lebanon than to any other country. According to the Census Bureau, there were over half a million Americans of Lebanese extraction—about a quarter of all Arab Americans—in the country in 2010. Egyptian Americans were the next largest Arab group, numbering about 190,000. They were followed by Syrian Americans (about 148,000), Iraqi Americans (about 106,000), and Palestinian Americans (about 93,000).

The Diversity Lottery

Foreigners wishing to enter the United States need to obtain a visa. There are many types of visas, but they fall into two broad categories: immigrant (for permanent residence) and non-immigrant (for work, travel, or study on a temporary basis). For countries with low immigration rates to the United States, Section 203 (c) of the Immigration and Nationality Act established the Diversity Immigrant Visa Lottery. Each year, the government makes available 50,000 permanent resident visas through a lottery drawing.

As with any lottery, there are many players but relatively few winners. According to the U.S. Department of State, of the 9,388,986 qualified applicants for the 2015 lottery, 125,514 were selected randomly to be in the lottery pool. Still, the "pay-

Middle Eastern immigrants hand out literature on Islam on a street in Toronto's Dundas Square.

off" is worth the long odds: permanent resident status and the ability to bring a husband or wife and any unmarried children under the age of 21 to the United States. The 2015 lottery pool included many people from the Middle East, among them 3,076 Algerians, 4,988 Egyptians, 2,844 Moroccans, and 3,484 Sudanese.

Middle Eastern Immigration to Canada

As was the case with the United States, Canada began receiving Middle Eastern immigrants in the late 1800s. At times in those early years, however, the response to some Middle Easterners, like Canadian winters, was somewhat chilly. "Around the turn of the century, there were fears that these Arab-origin immigrants, along with immigrants from Asia and Eastern and Southern Europe, would negatively affect Canada's Anglo-Saxon heritage and white European master project," write Sharon McIrvin Abu-Laban and Baha Abu-Laban in Arabs in America: Building a New Future. "Consequently, Arab immigrants faced serious barriers in their admission, were characterized harshly by ranking officials of the time, and were viewed as difficult to assimilate into the Canadian ideal."

Today, immigrants are recognized as being essential to Canada's economic future, and because of that, Canada has put out the welcome mat. The government encourages its citizens to volunteer in a Host Program, in which they show new immigrants around their community, help them become familiar with local businesses and schools, and introduce them to Canadian culture.

According to Canada's 2011 census, more than 660,000 Canadians claimed Arab ethnic origins, alone or in combination with some other ethnicity. The vast majority of them lived in the provinces of Quebec and Ontario. Canada was also home to more than 163,000 residents of full or partial Iranian ancestry, with major communities in Ontario, Quebec, and British Columbia. Just 15,000 Canadians claimed Israeli heritage.

In her book *Saffron Sky: A Life Between Iran and America*,

Iranian American journalist Gelareh Asayesh explained why her parents, who immigrated to the United States from Iran in 1977, eventually settled in Canada. "In Canada, where immigrants were not the problem they had become in the United States, and where the Iranian hostage crisis was not a personal affront, my parents felt welcome in a way they had not in America," Asayesh said. "Winnipeg offered a warm and friendly Iranian community. . . . Canada offered my parents what the United States never had: the promise of permanence."

 # Text-Dependent Questions

1. Identify some of the factors that led to the first wave of Middle Eastern immigration to the United States.
2. How did the 1991 Gulf War adversely affect Palestinians?
3. What were the Oslo Accords?

 # Research Project

It has long been assumed that the Israeli-Palestinian conflict will end only with a "two-state solution"—that is, the creation of an independent Palestinian state existing alongside Israel. But the two sides have never been able to agree on specific terms. Among the most difficult issues are: where the borders of a Palestinian state should be drawn; who should control Jerusalem, which Israel claims as its capital but which the Palestinians believe rightfully belongs to them; and how (or even whether) Palestinians displaced from their land by past wars should be compensated. Research the claims made by each side. Then imagine yourself a neutral mediator between Israel and the Palestinians. Outline the compromises you would want each side to make for peace. Make sure to explain your reasoning.

4 MAKING A NEW LIFE

Middle Eastern immigrants often live in the traditional havens for newcomers—large cities such as New York, Los Angeles, and Toronto. On the other hand, because education is a common pull factor, it's not unusual to find small Middle Eastern enclaves near college towns. According to the Arab American Institute, one-third of Arab Americans live in New York, California, or Michigan. An additional one-third live in the seven states with the next largest Arab American populations. They are (in descending order): Texas, Florida, Illinois, New Jersey, Ohio, Massachusetts, and Pennsylvania.

California has by far the largest Iranian American population. New York, Texas, Maryland, and Virginia also have significant Iranian American communities.

Notable Middle Eastern Communities in the United States

Perhaps the most well known hub for Middle Eastern Americans is metropolitan Detroit, especially Dearborn, Michigan, which is located southwest of the Motor City. Today, more than 30 percent of Dearborn's approximately 95,000 residents are Arab Americans.

◀Students of the American Islamic Academy in Dearborn, Michigan, attend a banquet. During the early part of the 20th century, Arab immigrants were attracted to Dearborn (headquarters of the Ford Motor Company) by well-paying jobs in the automobile industry. Today the Detroit-Dearborn area is home to one of the nation's largest and most important Arab American communities.

Detroit's Arab American community dates back to the late 1800s, when some of the first Middle Eastern immigrants to the United States, primarily Lebanese men, worked as peddlers. As the automobile industry developed and grew in the early 20th century, however, many Arab immigrants found work in the factories. (These jobs were more plentiful for immigrants because of the Ford Motor Company's policy against hiring blacks to work in its auto plants.) "The Arab American community gradually concentrated in the Dearborn row houses constructed by Henry Ford, literally in the shadows of the Rouge plant," writes Karen Rignall in "Building an Arab-American Community in Dearborn," an article published in the *Journal of the International Institute*.

Over the years, people from other Middle Eastern countries have come to southeast Michigan: Yemenis, Syrians, Palestinians, and many more. "Each wave of arrivals adds another layer to the rich history of this heterogeneous community," says Rignall. "Arab immigrants hope Dearborn will offer chances of finding work. They also look to Dearborn for social networks, mosques and churches where they may pray in a familiar manner, stores where they may buy the clothes they prefer and the foods they grew up with: in sum, a cultural milieu that dulls the edges of the experience of dislocation and adjustment."

New York City, a magnet for immigrants from all over the world, is home to a sizable community of Syrian Jews. It's believed that up to 75,000 New York residents belong to this somewhat unusual Arab-Jewish group (though it's difficult to

 Words to Understand in This Chapter

bachelor's degree—an undergraduate degree from a college or university.
enclave—a community that is culturally or ethnically different from the surrounding area.
heterogeneous—made up of diverse or dissimilar elements.

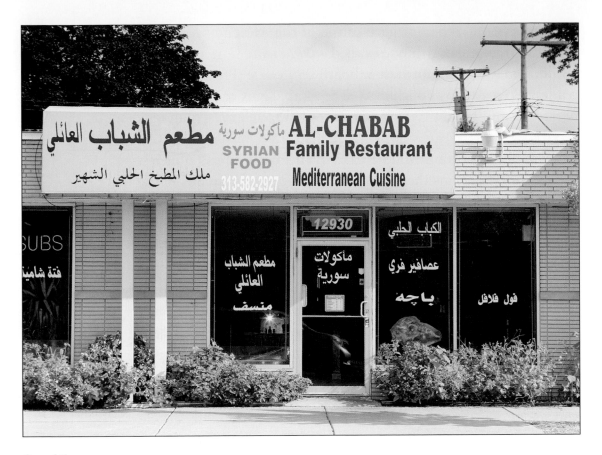

One of the many Arab businesses in the greater Detroit area. Dearborn has one of the highest concentrations of Arab people outside of the Middle East.

pinpoint a precise figure because Syrian Jews don't usually identify themselves as Arabs or Jewish Arabs). While many Syrian Jews live in Brooklyn's Flatbush and Bensonhurst neighborhoods, some have migrated to New Jersey.

The casual observer wouldn't notice much, if any, difference between the Syrian Jews and other Jewish groups in Brooklyn, according to Walter P. Zenner, who has studied this community since the late 1950s. "But there are ways in which they have in the past and continue today to maintain aspects of their Middle Eastern heritage," writes Zenner in *A Community of Many Worlds: Arab Americans in New York City.*

Of particular note is the music in their services. "The most Arab of cultural forms for Syrian Jews in Brooklyn is paradoxically one of the most Jewish," says Zenner. "The Syrian Jewish community has preserved Arab music for use with Hebrew songs and prayers. . . . The liturgical music of the Aleepan synagogue follows Arab musical modes called *maqamaat*. One particular mode, *sikah*, is used for most Sabbath services and for the Torah reading." As Zenner concludes, "The Arabic musical tradition is preserved and taught to new generations through the synagogue service."

Another important Middle Eastern enclave is in Los Angeles. In fact, L.A. contains the largest concentration of Iranians in the world outside of Iran itself. An estimated 500,000 Iranians live in Southern California; many of them immigrated around the time of Iran's Islamic Revolution in 1979. According to an Associated Press article, "Iranians Make Home in L.A.," the tastes and sounds of Iran are found easily in the city some Iranian Americans refer to as "Tehrangeles." "Along Westwood Boulevard and in the San Fernando Valley, signs in Farsi's delicate, cursive script advertise Persian market rug merchants, restaurants serving a staple rice-and-meat dish called chello kebab and grocery stores stocking biranyi paste, lavash bread and halva, a nougat made with sesame seeds," the article reports. Although immigrants might find these familiar things comforting, one young Iranian American notes that the youth "love anything that's American."

Working in America

Middle Eastern immigrants tend to be well educated—in 2013, according to data from the U.S. Census Bureau, 43 percent of those age 25 and older had a bachelor's degree or higher—and they are represented in virtually every field, including medicine, education, finance, the arts, and the automobile industry. It was the auto industry that drew many of the first wave of Arab immigrants to the greater Detroit area. Some have made the transition from line workers to labor officials. The late Stephen Yokich, who served two terms as president of the United Auto Workers, was of Arab descent.

Like other immigrants, many Middle Eastern newcomers are self-employed. Some Middle Eastern businesses have grown into

From Her Kitchen to Yours

As a girl growing up in Baghdad, Iraq, Nawal Nasrallah loved the smells wafting from her family's and her neighbors' kitchens. Today, she helps bring those aromas into American kitchens. She is the author of *Delights from the Garden of Eden: A Cookbook and a History of the Iraqi Cuisine*, a compilation of recipes and food-related stories from Mesopotamia, an area that gave rise to some of the world's oldest civilizations.

An accomplished cook and a thorough researcher, Nasrallah shares traditional recipes such as appetizers, vegetarian dishes, and desserts. The book also has an ample dash of Iraqi history and culture. For example, it explains that Italian cannoli, a tubular pastry shell filled with sweetened ricotta cheese, has culinary ancestors: a 10th-century Iraqi sweet called *halaqeem* and a 13th-century treat known as *qanawat*—literally, "a tube."

Nasrallah presents a culinary journey in her cookbook, but her personal journey to the United States is even more compelling. Her husband, Shakir Mustafa, came to North America in 1990 to earn his doctorate; the family, Nasrallah and three children—Shamam, Iba, and Bilal—planned to join him soon afterward. The day they were to leave, however, Iraqi soldiers invaded Kuwait. Shamam, as an 18-year-old male, was forced to stay behind, but the others managed to get a ride with a truck driver to Amman, Jordan. From there they flew to New York and, ultimately, to Indiana, where Mustafa was studying. After about a year, Shamam was able to rejoin the family.

Nasrallah, who was a professor of English literature before coming to the United States, worked as a seamstress to support the family, but she never lost her interest in research and food.

In 1996 tragedy struck the family. Bilal, the youngest child, suffered a fatal brain hemorrhage. The cookbook was a way for Nasrallah to work through the loss of her 13-year-old son.

On a broader level, notes Nasrallah, the book introduces Iraq's cuisine and its rich cultural traditions to Westerners, including second- and third-generation Iraqi Americans. After the 1991 Gulf War, many families left Iraq, she says, which gave rise to a whole generation growing up away from their home country. Many of them are not able to read Arabic, and yet they need to know something about their heritage. "This is where my cookbook comes in," she says, adding that her daughter, Iba, a lawyer, used to call her and ask how to prepare her favorite traditional dishes. That was not easy, given the lengthy explanations required. "Now, I tell her what page to turn to in my book, and spend the rest of the call chatting."

large, well-known enterprises, such as the Haggar Clothing Company or the Maloof Companies, which, among other ventures, operates hotels and casinos. But other Middle Eastern businesses are small: mom-and-pop stores, gas stations, restaurants.

Home Away from Home

Being a recently arrived immigrant and being the new kid in school have something in common: It helps to have someone show the way around. For some Middle Eastern immigrants, that someone will be a family member.

Community organizations also can play an important role. In Dearborn, the Arab Community Center for Economic and Social Services (ACCESS) runs a variety of programs serving tens of thousands of people each year. ACCESS "started off helping men find industrial jobs by teaching them the English words for wrench, hammer, nail, saw, and other tools," according to an article in the April 2003 issue of the magazine *Washington Report on Middle East Affairs*. "Next it gave Arab women English lessons. Before long ACCESS was providing all kinds of human services, including helping immigrants start small businesses and navigate the school, banking, health care and social

An Iranian-American woman participates in the 2015 Norooz Festival and Persian Parade in Los Angeles, California. More Iranians live in the Los Angeles area than anywhere else in the world outside of Iran—leading some expatriates to dub their adopted hometown "Tehrangeles."

and civil systems most Americans take for granted." ACCESS, which won a Points of Light Award in 1992, has an extensive cultural arts program as well. One of its largest endeavors, the Arab American National Museum, opened in 2005.

In addition to family and community centers, the synagogues, churches, and mosques that serve communities with large Middle Eastern immigrant populations often take on a dual role: religious center and socialization outlet. In "Expressions of Islam in America," Gisela Webb, a professor of religious studies, notes that some mosques, much like some urban ethnic churches, "function as centers for learning and sharing information about surviving in America as much as they are centers for prayer."

 Text-Dependent Questions

1. What drew Arab immigrants to the Detroit area in the early years of the 20th century?
2. Which American city is home to a large community of Syrian Jews?
3. Around which U.S. city are Iranian Americans heavily concentrated?

 Research Project

Choose a Middle Eastern country. Then, using the Internet, see if you can find out approximately how many people living in your city, state, or province are immigrants from that country.

5 FITTING IN

Assimilation, in simple terms, is the process by which a person from one culture takes on the mind-set, habits, and customs of another culture. While Arab Americans have generally done very well for themselves, noted scholar Michael Suleiman believes that they still haven't been fully accepted in the United States. "True integration and full assimilation have eluded them," Suleiman asserts in Arabs in America: Building a New Future.

Like some Arabs in North America, some Israelis have not assimilated into the larger society—and don't want to. In her article "The New Immigrants: A Contemporary Profile," Rina Cohen examines Israelis living in Canada. Cohen suggests that Israeli Canadians "feel guilty for leaving their homeland and express significant ambivalence about their presence in Canada. Most of them foster a dream to return to Israel one day. Thus, they make no visible efforts to assimilate into the culture of the country in which they live, or even into that of the native Jewish community."

In fact, Cohen notes, Israeli Jews in Toronto "have deliberately distanced themselves from the highly organized Jewish community, constituting an Israeli ethnic group in the city."

◀ An Arab American family at the dinner table. The experiences and attitudes of Middle Eastern immigrants are likely to differ markedly from those of their North American-born children, and typically the grandchildren of immigrants are fully assimilated into Canadian or American culture.

Perhaps some of this desire to remain separate from the larger Jewish community reflects the differing attitudes toward religion held by Israeli immigrants: whereas Canadian Jews, Cohen observes, tend to emphasize the religious significance of Judaism, Israeli immigrants tend to have a more nationalistic view of what it means to be Jewish. "In order to escape both assimilation and religiosity, Israelis take action to maintain cultural connections with Israel and other Israelis," notes Cohen.

Naama Sabar studied an interesting subset of Israeli immigrants: kibbutzniks living in Los Angeles. (A kibbutz is a communal settlement in Israel; the people who live in a kibbutz are called kibbutzniks.) The kibbutzniks don't fit the typical profile of Israeli American immigrants: they're not as well-off or as educated, they tend to be self-employed, and the women work outside the home.

Kibbutzniks are not exempt from problems such as culture shock or language difficulties, Sabar notes; they just handle these challenges differently from other immigrants. "What helps them cope with the changes in their lives is the highly developed social network which serves as a security net, a mechanism of survival. This social network is characterized by multiple, intense, substantial personal links based on friendship, interdependence, and mutual background, rather than the official organizations which characterize other immigrant groups in the United States," observes Sabar in her book *Kibbutzniks in the Diaspora*. "The kibbutzniks cope with their foreignness by creating an 'island of estrangement.'"

 Words to Understand in This Chapter

first generation—people born in one country who move to another.

Koran—the holy book of Islam; also spelled Qur'an.

second generation—the children of immigrants born in the country to which their parents immigrated.

Orthodox Jews participate in a service at 770 Eastern Parkway, headquarters of the Chabad-Lubavitch Hasidic movement in Brooklyn's Crown Heights neighborhood.

Arguably, assimilation can be somewhat easier for immigrants who came to North America because they wanted to than for those who felt they had no choice but to immigrate. Many Palestinians fall into the latter group. "Palestine, the homeland and the nostalgic village, is alive in Palestinian memories and viewed as the utopian solution," writes May Seikaly in *Arabs in America: Building a New Future*. "On the whole, this community sees itself as transplanted, forced into exile by conditions beyond its control. To mitigate the effect of this alienation, Palestinians in America transplant the lifestyle of the old country. . . . They surround themselves with the artifacts of the culture: embroideries, the mounted religious drawings and scripts, the sounds of Arabic music and language, and the smells of Arab food."

Similarly, Iranian culture is emotionally binding and nationalistic, says Ali Akbar Mahdi in "The Second Generation

Iranians: Questions and Concerns." However, "while the Iranian immigrants often express a strong desire for preservation of their cultural heritage, they show no resistance to the forces of assimilation to the host society." Although Iranian Americans are relatively large in number and live in major cities such as Los Angeles, Mahdi believes that "it is still too early to speak of the Iranian community in the U.S. as a national phenomenon" and says that "it is not very clear to what extent the Iranians have been able to transfer their cultural heritage to their children."

Palestinians protest in New York City against Israel's occupation of the West Bank.

Age to Age

Mahdi raises an important point: the experiences of immigrants and their children (and grandchildren and great-grandchildren) vary significantly. People who emigrated from their country of birth as adults—referred to as first-generation immigrants—typically have a more difficult time adapting to life in their new country than do children born in the new country (referred to as the second generation). For example, a Sudanese couple who immigrate to the United States in their twenties may have difficulty mastering the English language or learning the nuances of Western culture. But their American-born children will almost inevitably learn English in school and absorb American attitudes and customs from their peers—even if their parents continue to speak Nubian and observe other Sudanese customs at home. In turn, the third generation (the grandchildren of the original immigrants) will probably be even more "Americanized"; indeed, they may have little if any knowledge of, or interest in, the "old country." As Mahdi notes, "While the first generation immigrants make every effort to maintain the native language and culture, the second generation's efforts in learning parental language and culture are very limited and half-hearted. The third generation's efforts in this regard are very minimal and symbolic. By fourth generation, little of a grandparent's cultural heritage can be found."

In many ways, members of the "1.5 generation"—as those who immigrate (usually with their parents) during childhood or the early teen years are sometimes called—encounter the most vexing situations from a cultural standpoint. They are, in a sense, between two cultures. One young Iranian American describes it this way: "They have a word in Persian, 'do-hava.' It means 'two-weathered.' You're not completely American and not completely Iranian."

East vs. West

The Arab Americans who have recently immigrated to the United States are quite different from those who came more than 100 years ago. The first arrivals typically desired to fit in with the American way of life; that's not necessarily so with today's newcomers. Yvonne Yazbeck Haddad, in *A Community of Many Worlds: Arab Americans in New York City*, notes, "The new immigrants tend to be more ethnically conscious, have more contact with the home country, and in general are more protective of their religious identity."

The clash between Western and Middle Eastern cultures sometimes plays out in the classroom. Paula Hajar, of Columbia University's Teachers College, surveyed Arab American parents and their children's teachers. The teachers expressed concern about gender inequality, corporal punishment, and the Arab mothers' lack of involvement in the schools. From the parents' perspective, teachers were viewed as weak disciplinarians who held low academic expectations for their students. "When a teacher was more concerned with 'being a friend to [the] child'

 ## Fascinating Rhythms

When Scott Marcus's orchestra members begin to play, the distinctive sounds of the *ud* and *saz*; *nay*; and *qanun* and *santur* fill the air, with the *dumbek*, *darabukkah*, and *zarb* keeping the beat. These Arab and Turkish lutes, reed flutes, plucked and hammered zithers, and percussion instruments, respectively, do more than play Middle Eastern music; in the hands of Marcus's Middle East Ensemble, they promote cultural harmony.

The Middle East Ensemble at the University of California–Santa Barbara—America's largest Middle Eastern orchestra—includes a chorus and a dance troupe. A few of the Ensemble's 60-plus members are from the Middle East, but most are Americans. Their concerts draw from a rich and diverse well of Arab, Armenian, Persian, Turkish, and Greek music and dance, from folk songs to modern tunes to classical music. "And yet classical Middle Eastern music isn't reserved for a few," observes Marcus, an ethnomusicologist who has studied in Egypt and is a professor at UCSB. "It's accessible to everyone and known by people on the street."

Middle Eastern music can't be described in simple terms, says Marcus. For example, there are several types of Egyptian music, and each country's music has its own distinctive rhythm. "The rhythm is part of the cultural identity," he says. While the traditional Western octave has 12 notes, the Middle Eastern octave has 24 notes and includes half flats and half sharps.

The Middle East Ensemble's concerts have reached people as close by as California and as far away as Uzbekistan, where the group performed at the Festival of Eastern Song. Some audiences enjoy the sounds and dances of their homelands; for others, it's a new experience. "The Ensemble's concerts present the diversity and dynamism of Middle Eastern cultures in an entertaining and educational way," says Marcus. "We introduce a dance or a song so that audience members not only listen to or see the performance, but so that they have a better appreciation for the cultural themes. We break down a lot of stereotypes."

rather than keeping the child in line or making demands on him or her," Hajar notes, "parents were distressed. They did, however, appreciate the American way of teaching to many different abilities and not just attending to the academically gifted, which was often the case in their own countries."

Is Sisterhood Powerful?

Many North Americans believe that in the Islamic societies of the Middle East, women are second-class citizens, oppressed and relegated solely to traditional roles such as wife and mother. Many Middle Eastern women, in turn, believe that this stereotype is inaccurate and unfair. Islam's holy book, the Koran, is fairly straightforward when it comes to the question of women's status in society: woman, it says, "enjoys equal rights to those of man in everything, she stands on an equal footing with men." Yet Arab culture traditionally has accorded men superior status.

Today, the rights and status of Middle Eastern women vary considerably by country. For example, Israel and Turkey, which are not Arab countries, generally guarantee equal rights to women under the law. In Iran, which also is not an Arab country, a woman may not travel abroad or work outside the home without the permission of her husband; when in public Iranian women are required to wear conservative Islamic dress, such as the chador, a dark cloak that covers the entire body except for the face. Women are not permitted to drive a car in Saudi Arabia. In Yemen, they may not leave the house without the permission of their husband or a male relative.

One highly visible symbol of the way society's image of women (and women's self-image) differs in Western and Islamic Middle Eastern cultures is the wearing of the traditional head covering, or *hijab*. Muslim women who wear the *hijab* say it's their choice—and a liberating one, at that. "In the Western world, the *hijab* has come to symbolize either forced silence or radical, unconscionable militancy," writes Naheed Mustafa, a Canadian Muslim, in "My Body Is My Own Business." "Actually, it is neither. It is simply a woman's assertion that judgment of her physical person is to play no role whatsoever in social interaction."

Not all Muslim American women share the same feelings about wearing the *hijab*. For his study, Ali Akbar Mahdi surveyed first-generation Iranian American female immigrants: 73 percent said the veil limited movement, and 80 percent strongly disagreed that it was good protection for women. Mahdi's 113-question survey spanned topics from Islamic law to marriage. Overall, concludes Mahdi, while many of these women disagree with the Iranian traditional role of women, few identify themselves as feminists in the Western definition. "Although these women believe in male-female equality and in the opportunities provided to women to enhance their status in society, they are not too enthusiastic about the individualistic demands characterizing Western feminism," Mahdi says.

Ways of the Middle East

Just as Middle Eastern immigrants bring with them long-standing habits, they also preserve the arts and holidays that are important to them. One Middle Eastern art that is treasured and practiced by many immigrants is calligraphy, writing in beautiful, stylized script. There are many forms of Arabic calligraphy, which is written from right to left. Calligraphy has special significance to Muslims: because of the traditional Islamic prohibition against depicting the human form, calligraphy has been used to adorn everything from books to mosques.

Many Middle Eastern immigrants continue to observe the major holy days of their faith: for Jews, Passover and Yom Kippur; for Muslims, Ramadan, a month of fasting; and for Christians, Christmas and Easter. They may also observe a special new year according to their own calendar, such as Rosh Hashanah for the Jews. Yet, particularly if the immigrants are living apart from others with the same cultural or religious background, a holiday might lose some of its significance.

Iranian American journalist Gelareh Asayesh hadn't observed the Iranian calendar since her teens. But that changed

Canadian Muslims wear headscarves while attending an Islamic Cultural Expo in Vancouver. Some Westerners view the *hijab* as a symbol of the repression women endure in Middle Eastern Islamic societies. But many Muslim women disagree, and they continue to wear the traditional headscarf even after moving to North America.

after the birth of her daughter, she writes in *Saffron Sky: A Life Between Iran and America*. Iranian holidays include Charshanbeh-soori, or "festive Wednesday," a farewell to winter; and Sizdah-bedar, observed on the 13th day of the new year, to ward off bad luck. But it's the Iranian New Year, Norooz, that has major significance, complete with presents, parties, and a *haft-sin* (literally, seven objects that begin with the letter *s*). "The *haft-sin*, the functional equivalent of the Christmas tree or the menorah, is a metaphor for life, a collection of symbolic objects laid out for the New Year," Asayesh explains, listing the items and their significance. "Greens and apples and Russian olives for abundance, gold coins for prosperity, hyacinth for beauty, vinegar and garlic for life's bitter moments."

Followers of some Middle Eastern Christian faiths observe St. Barbara's Day in December. As the story is told, Barbara was the daughter of a pagan, Dioscurus, who locked her in a tower

and then killed her because of her conversion to Christianity. Upon her death, Dioscurus was struck by lightning and reduced to a pile of ashes. Some Middle Eastern children dress in costume on this day and collect treats, making the holiday similar to Halloween. One traditional dish, *Burbura* (Arabic for Barbara) is a pudding that includes shelled wheat and apricots, a reminder of what the patron saint of miners and firefighters had to eat when she was locked in the tower.

Islam in North America

The earliest Arab immigrants to the United States were Christian, but many who have come after 1965 are Muslim. Because neither the Census Bureau nor the Bureau of Citizenship and Immigration Services collects religious information in its data, it's difficult to determine the number of American Muslims. The Pew Research Center estimated that in 2015, there

Arab American girls at an Islamic summer school in Pasadena, California, where all instruction is conducted in the Arabic language. Many immigrants from the Middle East consider it vital that they pass on their cultural traditions and native tongue to their children.

were 3.3 million Muslims of all ages in the United States, meaning Muslims constituted about 1 percent of the total U.S. population. By midcentury, Pew projects, the Muslim population will be 8.1 million, or 2.1 percent of the U.S. population.

Immigration has played a huge role in the growth of Islam in the United States. A 2014 Pew survey found that 63 percent of American Muslims were immigrants. A large share came from the Middle East, and that trend is expected to continue in the coming decades.

According to Gisela Webb's article "Expressions of Islam in America," some mosques take on a distinctive Western flavor. "Adaptations were made to conform to American church patterns, such as scheduling congregational prayers on Sundays and allowing 'mixed' (men and women) social functions, such as dances," she writes. These practices have been frowned upon by more recent Muslim arrivals, who tend to hold more conservative beliefs.

Webb says a conflict sometimes exists between certain Muslim practices and Western culture. "In general, Muslims in America who have been raised in traditional Muslim cultures speak of the tension they experience in trying to remain close to linguistic, cultural, ethnic, and religious roots while trying to develop a sense of belonging in their adopted home," she says. "Work schedules do not easily allow for the five-times-daily salat prayers or Friday congregational prayers. Institutional eating facilities (schools, prisons, military) are not set up for Muslim dietary practices. The pervasiveness of alcohol in America and the cultural acceptance of sexual permissiveness and immodesty . . . are seen as negative influences on the faith community, particularly on its young people."

And as Yvonne Yazbeck Haddad mentions in *A Community of Many Worlds: Arab Americans in New York City*, "They [Muslims] soon become aware that the public school system is geared to eradicate immigrant culture, and that it has generally been successful in this endeavor through long school days that incorporate co-educational activities such as swimming, dancing, acting, hobbies, and trips (which often violate Muslim desires for separation of the sexes)."

Language—Living or Lost

Many Arabic dialects, or regional language variations, exist in the Middle East—sometimes within the same country. It's understandable, then, that there are variations in the Arabic spoken by Arabs in North America. Take for example, the Arabic word *mabsoot*: Iraqis use it to mean physically beaten; to the Lebanese, it means happy. "Many Arabs simply cannot communicate with each other because they cannot understand each other's dialects. . . . For all, the common language is English," writes Yvonne Yazbeck Haddad in *A Community of Many Worlds: Arab Americans in New York City*.

Margaret Salome, a linguist, identifies three categories of immigrants who tend to retain their native tongue: those who are of lower socioeconomic status; those who live in minority neighborhoods with many other speakers of the language; and those with a great deal of ethnic pride. A Yemeni community in upstate New York that speaks primarily Arabic exemplifies the first category. "Members of that community became laborers with low levels of income and education. Therefore, the socioeconomic homogeneity formerly shared in Yemen continues in the United States; it encourages isolation from mainstream America, and it makes it easier for members to retain language, culture, and traditions," observes Salome in *Food for Our Grandmothers: Writings by Arab-American and Arab-Canadian Feminists*.

There's a connection between the number of language speakers and the rate of retention: When many people are speaking the language at social events and in business circles, the tongue lives on. Salome points to the Cuban American community in Miami as an example. "You can spend your life in this community, go to work, run a business, and never speak English," she notes.

Salome interviewed the coordinator of an Arabic-language school in Seattle. "Members of the Arabic-language speaking community are committed to the school; it's part of a larger project involving the creation of an Arab culture center," she reports. "Community members believe a primary benefit for their children will be a sense of pride in Arabic culture and heritage."

For Berbers, retaining their mother tongue, Tamazight, is a way of preserving their culture, even if they are on foreign soil. The few thousand Berbers living in the United States are not generally located in one particular area, says Arezki Boudif, a researcher in chemistry and president of the Amazigh Cultural Association in America (ACAA). "Teaching our children our language and culture is not easy because we are so spread out," he says. So, ACAA members have multi-state events, like the celebration of the Berber spring, where traditional songs are sung and poetry is read. ACAA also maintains a multi-location resource center, sponsors concerts and seminars, publishes a newsletter, and even helps people acquire Berber music that's hard to find in the United States.

 # Text-Dependent Questions

1. What is a kibbutznik?
2. To whom does the term 1.5 generation refer?
3. What is Tamazight?

 # Research Project

Investigate a holiday observed in a Middle Eastern culture or country. Write a one-page report about the holiday. Make sure to explain the holiday's significance and to describe the customs and traditions associated with its observance.

6 STEREOTYPES, DISCRIMINATION, AND OTHER PROBLEMS

Even before the September 11, 2001, terrorist attacks, some Middle Eastern immigrants—especially Muslims and Arabs—had experienced the sting of racism. A string of international incidents fed the image of Muslims and Arabs as violent, anti-Western and anti-American fanatics. A partial list of these incidents includes the murder, by Palestinian terrorists, of Israeli athletes at the 1972 Summer Olympics in Munich, West Germany; the Iran hostage crisis (1979 to 1981); the 1983 suicide truck-bomb attack on the barracks of U.S. Marine peacekeepers in Beirut, Lebanon, which killed 241 servicemen and was believed to have been carried out by the Iran-backed Islamist group Hezbollah; the 1985 hijacking of the Italian cruise ship Achille Lauro, during which Palestinian terrorists murdered a wheelchair-bound American Jew and dumped his body overboard; the 1988 bombing of a Pan Am jetliner over Lockerbie, Scotland, which claimed 270 lives and was linked to the Libyan government; the 1993 bombing of the World Trade Center by Islamic fundamentalists with links to al-Qaeda; and the al-Qaeda-sponsored bombings of American embassies in Kenya and Tanzania in 1998, which resulted in more than 200 deaths and 4,000 injuries. In the wake of these and other out-

◀ A demonstrator holds a sign opposing the admission of refugees from Syria and other Middle Eastern countries to the United States at a 2015 demonstration in Boise, Idaho. The issue was hotly debated during the 2016 presidential election campaign.

rages, some Americans viewed Middle Easterners as a group with fear, distrust, and hostility—even though there is no evidence to suggest that significant numbers of Middle Eastern immigrants support the actions of violent extremists.

But stereotypes are often hard to dispel. And, in the opinion of some experts, harmful stereotypes of Arabs, Arab Americans, and Muslims have long been perpetuated in American popular culture. Media critic Jack G. Shaheen examined more than 900 motion pictures, from the early days of Hollywood to the present, for his book *Reel Bad Arabs: How Hollywood Vilifies a People*. Among the recurring stereotypes he noted were that Arabs are primitive and fanatical and place little value on human life. Shaheen, who is also the author of *The TV Arabs*, believes that on the small screen Arabs are stereotyped as "billionaires, bombers and belly dancers." But, he writes in *A Community of Many Worlds: Arab Americans in New York City*, what is most disturbing about television movies and programs with Arab characters "is that they effectively show all Arabs, Muslims, and Arab Americans as being at war with the United States."

Living in the Shadow of September 11

Not surprisingly, the terrorist acts of September 11, 2001, stirred powerful emotions among Americans. In the minds of a small number of people, the violence and pain inflicted on the victims and their families justified vigilante-style revenge against Arab and Muslim Americans. Between September 11, 2001, and October 1, 2001, the U.S. Commission on Civil Rights received

 Words to Understand in This Chapter

hate crime—a usually violent crime that is motivated by bias against a group to which the victim belongs (for example, his or her race, ethnicity, religion, or sexual orientation).

ostracism—exclusion from social acceptance.

overstays—foreigners who remain in a country longer than their visa permits.

In the immediate aftermath of the September 11, 2001, attacks on the World Trade Center and Pentagon, Arab and Muslim Americans lived under a pall of suspicion.

692 reports of ethnic intimidation; more than half were directed toward Arab Americans. Because of underreporting, the actual number of incidents may be significantly higher.

Hateful words and slashed tires were among the lesser offenses. An Indiana man repeatedly rammed his car into a mosque, and a Muslim woman wearing traditional headdress was punched while waiting for a bus. According to the Civil Rights Commission, she was asked, "Where are you going? To mosque, to bombing classes?" A Sikh gas station owner, mistaken for a Muslim, was shot and killed.

The hate crimes were widely condemned. The Civil Rights Commission ran a public service announcement encouraging tolerance, and several state governments organized public forums. David Shaheed, an Indiana judge, told the Civil Rights

Commission, "These [hate] incidents were limited and merely a trifling annoyance compared to the outpouring of concern by leaders of government and the faith communities to see that Muslims and people of Middle Eastern appearance were not unjustly targeted for abuse and attack."

However, in the 11 months after the attacks, the U.S. Department of Justice detained hundreds of Middle Easterners on immigration violations such as overstaying their visas or entering the United States illegally, as the government sought to identify possible terrorists. Some detainees were held for eight months or more without being charged with a crime.

A report by the Justice Department's Office of the Inspector General, released in June 2003, criticized the treatment of some detainees, saying they were physically and verbally abused by prison guards while being held in excessively harsh conditions— at times in maximum security, wearing leg shackles. The report acknowledged that the chaos and uncertainty that followed the attacks made the Justice Department's job more difficult, but it said not all of the abuses could be excused. The department stood by its policies as necessary to protect the country from further attacks.

 From Lost Boys to Found Men

Many Americans became aware of the long-running Sudanese civil war only after hearing about the plight of the Lost Boys of Sudan.

Fighting between the Sudanese military and the Sudan People's Liberation Army (SPLA) erupted in 1983; by the time a peace agreement was signed in 2005, the war had led to the deaths of an estimated 2 million people. Many Sudanese children lost their parents or were separated from their families. By 1987 an estimated 20,000 young people, mostly boys from the Dinka and Nuer tribes, began a trek for survival, walking hundreds of miles in search of a safe haven from the fighting and, in many cases, for food. Many died during that quest; the luckier ones found their way to refugee camps, first in Ethiopia and later in Kenya.

About 3,400 of the Lost Boys—who are now young men—have settled in the United States, the result of a 1999 U.S.–United Nations agreement.

In June 2002 the Bush administration announced what quickly became a controversial set of immigration regulations: the National Security Entry-Exit Registration System. Attorney General John Ashcroft said, "This system will expand substantially America's scrutiny of those foreign visitors who may pose a national security concern and enter our country. And it will provide a vital line of defense in the war against terrorism." The system, which went into effect on September 11, 2002, required male nationals and citizens from certain countries to be fingerprinted, photographed, and registered with the U.S. government. Registration occurred in waves, with the first group called on being men from Iran, Iraq, Libya, Sudan, and Syria; the next group included men from Algeria, Bahrain, Lebanon, Morocco, Oman, Qatar, Tunisia, the United Arab Emirates, and Yemen; Saudi Arabian, Egyptian, Jordanian, and Kuwaiti men also were asked to register. (Men from certain non–Middle Eastern countries, such as North Korea and Pakistan, were also included in this registration.)

The new system's most controversial aspect became the detention of individuals who had pending applications with the Immigration and Naturalization Service, and the "call in" of many individuals for interviews at INS offices.

In June 2003, the Washington, D.C.–based Migration Policy Institute produced a report, with input from past Republican and Democratic INS commissioners, highly critical of a number of the immigration policies adopted after September 11. It criticized the "voluntary interview" program of Arabs and Muslims in the United States, noting, "The immigration enforcement focus [a number of people interviewed were detained] and public fanfare that surrounded the program worked against its potential for intelligence gathering." The report also stated that the "call-in special registration program has been poorly planned and has not achieved its objectives. Its goals have been contradictory: gathering information about non-immigrants [temporary visa holders] present in the United States, and deporting those with immigration violations. Many non-immigrants have rightly feared they will be detained or deported if they attempt to comply, so they have not registered. Moreover, any potential security benefits of registering people inside the United States will fade over time."

The report noted the "profound positive impact" of President Bush's visit to a Washington, D.C., mosque in the days after September 11. However, it also stated that many of the immigration-related measures taken have been "ineffective in responding to threats of terrorism, but are undertaken for political expediency or public relations at a huge price to" Arab and Muslim communities in the United States. The Migration Policy Institute report advocated greater emphasis on intelligence and information sharing and more cooperative engagement by law enforcement with Arab and Muslim communities.

In many cases, the government's search for terrorists resulted in the deportation of individuals for minor violations of immigration law. In January 2003, the *Atlanta Journal-Constitution* reported that deportees included "an Arab student in New York who was expelled for working seven hours a week beyond what his visa allowed and a Jordanian in New Jersey who violated terms of a tourist visa by working at a Dunkin' Donuts." The newspaper's computer analysis of INS data revealed that deportations to some Middle Eastern, North African, and South Asian countries more than doubled from October 2001 to September 2002, while the number of Mexican deportees dropped by nearly 25 percent.

By spring 2003, the Bush administration ended the special registration program, purportedly because it had accomplished its mission. All told, 130,000 men registered, 11,000 were questioned, and more than 2,300 were detained.

Attitudes Toward (and Attitudes of) Arab Americans and American Muslims

Events of the last couple decades—from al-Qaeda attacks and U.S. wars in the Middle East to the rise of ISIS—have contributed to some Americans' negative views of Arab Americans and Muslims generally. A December 2015 survey by the polling firm Zogby found that nearly one-third (30 percent) of American adults held an unfavorable opinion of Arab Americans, and 37 percent had an unfavorable opinion of American Muslims. Many of the survey's respondents wondered about the loyalties of Arab Americans and Muslims. When asked how they'd feel if an Arab American attained an important position in the U.S. government, 35 percent said the official's ethnicity would influence his or her decision making, while 37 percent expressed confidence the official could do the job. When asked the same question of Muslims, respondents were

Living the First Amendment

In his homeland of Egypt, says Tamer Melek, a Coptic Christian, wearing a crucifix necklace or attending church can be a "big problem." Christians may suffer discrimination ranging from the subtle (for example, being passed over for job promotions in favor of Muslims) to the flagrant (such as verbal harassment or even violence).

"Copts don't get the best jobs," says Melek, who was relegated to a low-level position in the Egyptian army once officials learned he was Christian. (Egyptians carry an identification card that includes religious affiliation.) "My father saw many younger Muslims with less experience getting promoted. The police stand guard outside the churches. The Muslim neighbors notice, too. They'll ask why you don't pray with them."

Melek had always wanted to travel, but his father persuaded him to finish his education first. And so he earned his college degree and served in the army, but there was one final barrier keeping him from leaving Egypt: finances. "To apply for a visa, you have to have money in the bank, about $25,000," he explains. "I didn't have the money, but I went to my uncle, a businessman, and told him of my situation. Much to my surprise, he agreed to put the money in the bank for me."

When Melek came to New York in 1996, he had a cousin and an aunt already in the United States to help him get acclimated. He also had another "family": members of an Egyptian Coptic church. They helped him avoid the pitfalls of immigration, such as unscrupulous lawyers or scam artists who take an unsuspecting client's money but don't take the necessary steps to keep the person in the country legally.

The mere existence of a Coptic church, without police officers present or harassment from onlookers, is to Melek a welcome miracle. "I can wear a cross—no problem. No one asks me, 'Why are you going to church?'" he says. "Here I can do whatever I want, and there are no problems."

An Islamic center in Dearborn, Michigan.

even more skeptical: just 31 percent were confident an American Muslim could do an important job in the government, while 46 percent believed Islam would color the official's decision making.

For their part, the overwhelming majority of Arab Americans and American Muslims are peace-loving, law abiding people who care deeply about their country. In a Gallup survey released in August 2011, for example, 89 percent of American Muslims said that violent attacks against civilians are never justified. Americans of other religious faiths were significantly less likely (between 10 percent and 18 percent) to categorically reject violence against civilians. In the same poll, two-thirds of American Muslims said they identified strongly with the United States. In a Zogby survey released in November 2014, more than 4 in 10 (43 percent) of Arab Americans said they'd experienced discrimination based on their ethnicity or country of origin. Still, 65 percent were confident life for their children would be better—and among first-generation Arab Americans that figure was 82 percent.

All in the Family

External forces such as racism and discrimination may not be the only difficulties Middle Easterners in North America face. The vastly different nature of Western society may also engender more subtle internal tensions. These struggles often play out between generations of the family. In *Arabs in America: Building a New Future*, sociologist Kristine Ajrouch writes about Arabic-speaking, Muslim students in a middle school in Dearborn, Michigan. Their parents, she notes, "are products of the traditional, agrarian culture of the Middle East, where the past is revered, there is emphasis on stability and conformity, and the elderly are held in high esteem because of their life experiences." By contrast, Ajrouch says, the children "are growing up in the technological, industrial culture of America. For them, the focus is on the future, not the past. Youth have higher status than the elderly, and emphasis is placed on personal achievement, rather than accumulated life experiences."

The Arab family has been described as patrilineal—that is, one where each member's rights and responsibilities are defined through the father. And yet, suggests Ajrouch, the family's honor pivots on the behavior of its female members, specifically their sexual conduct. "Chastity and honor," Ajrouch notes, "become imperative qualities for the female."

That being the case, it's not surprising that Arab young men are given a looser social rein than their sisters. A survey of Arab Canadian youth showed that even the younger generation adheres to traditional Arab attitudes toward women. Both teen males and teen females were asked to rate certain behaviors as favorable, unfavorable, or neutral. A young Arab man going out on dates, for example, was viewed as favorable by 62 percent of males and 53 percent of females. But a young Arab woman going out on dates was considered favorable by only 28 percent of males and 44 percent of females.

"The fact that dating and having a boyfriend or a girlfriend is considered normal and even desirable in American society prompts Arab parents to maintain a stronger hold on their daughters," writes Ajrouch. However, "the same standards and expectations that are levied on Arab girls are not applied to the non-Arab girls that the boys date."

For some Middle Eastern parents, the "anything goes" Western culture is just too much to handle. "Quite a number of Iranian parents have left this country because of their anxieties in raising their daughters in a culture with permissive sexual attitudes," writes Ali Akbar Mahdi in "The Second Generation Iranians: Questions and Concerns." "Some second generation youth," he adds, "are torn between trying to be what their parents want them to be and what the American society wants them to be. For some, these choices involve betrayal and ostracism, and a happy medium is hard, if not impossible, to achieve."

Middle Eastern American and Canadian immigrants tend to be stricter parents than is the Western norm, but that alone doesn't tell the whole family story. These families often spend a great deal of time together, with the mother spending the most time with her children. In the Arab Canadian teen survey, 69 percent of sons and 63 percent of daughters said they spent a considerable amount of time with their moms; only 59 percent of boys and 28 percent of girls said they spent a considerable amount of time with their dads. And even though much of these parent-child activities involved working around the house or shopping, about one-third of both male and female respondents said they wanted to spend more time with their parents. The Arab Canadian teens felt close to at least one parent; 9 of 10 who took the survey said they confided personally in their mother, father, or both parents.

Americans with an Eye on Their Birthplace

Not all Middle Easterners who come to North America intend to

Koran class, Dearborn, Michigan. Uncomfortable with what they perceive as the permissiveness of North American society, many Arab immigrants, particularly Muslims, want their children to follow the gender norms that prevail in their countries of origin.

make Canada or the United States their permanent home. Some complete their education and return to their homeland. Others wait for a stronger economy or for a more peaceful period in their country. Still others decide that the Western lifestyle clashes too much with their religious or cultural values.

John, a Sudanese refugee, was interviewed by Rogaia Mustafa Abusharaf, who said he described his experiences as "someone who is unexpectedly stranded away from home." At the time of the interview, John, who earned his Ph.D. in the United States, did not have a full-time job but was sending part of his salary to family in Sudan. He said, "I would like to go back to the Sudan once peace [and] racial, religious, and cultural equality is established. Because life here is not problem-free. Loneliness, stress, and racism are the most common problems."

Syrian refugees, with their meager possessions, arrive at a camp in Turkey.

Undocumented Immigrants and Refugees

In the United States, legal immigrants—foreign-born people who seek the right to live and work in the country permanently and have the proper documentation—must obtain a green card, or permanent resident visa. Green cards are issued by the Bureau of Citizenship and Immigration Services. A permanent resident need not seek to become an American citizen if he or she does not wish to. Compared with immigrants from other parts of the world, Middle Eastern immigrants have a higher U.S. citizenship rate than immigrants overall.

Not all foreign-born people living within U.S. borders are doing so legally. It was estimated that about 11 million people were in the United States illegally in early 2016. These people have entered the country without official documentation or permission, stayed longer in the country than their temporary visas allowed (referred to in immigration circles as "overstays"), or violated the terms of their visas (for example, by taking a job while in the country on a tourist visa). It's difficult to get a precise count of undocumented immigrants because, to state the obvious, few want to make their status known and risk deportation. However, based on government statistics, estimates of the number of Middle Easterners living in the United States illegally range from 100,000 to 200,000; Iran, Lebanon, and Jordan were among the top five source countries, according to U.S. government data.

The tougher stance on immigration that the United States adopted after September 11 drove many Middle Easterners living illegally in the United States to the Canadian border. Most were trying to beat the INS-imposed registration deadline for men from 25 Middle Eastern countries. They sought refugee status in Canada.

The U.S. Refugee Act of 1980 defines a refugee as "a person outside of his or her country of nationality who is unable or unwilling to return because of persecution or a well-founded fear of persecution on account of race, religion, nationality, membership in a particular social group, or political opinion."

According to UNHCR, the UN's refugee agency, there were 19.5 million refugees worldwide at the end of 2014. By that year, Syria had become the largest source country for refugees.

In the United States, the president—in consultation with Congress—sets an annual ceiling for the number of refugees that may be admitted into the country. From 2013 to 2015, the refugee ceiling was 70,000. In 2016, President Barack Obama proposed raising the ceiling to 85,000.

In previous years, Iraq had been among the leading source countries for refugees accepted into the United States. For 2016, President Obama proposed to dramatically increase the number of Syrian refugees admitted into the country, but that proposal generated opposition from Republicans in Congress, who said they were concerned about the possibility that ISIS fighters might slip into the country by pretending to be refugees from Syria's civil war.

For refugees, life in their new country, especially at first, can be difficult. In her article "Meet Your Brother with a Welcoming Smile—Refugees in America," Anne Marie Weiss-Armush writes about a Turkish Kurd refugee, Rukeiya, who came to the United States in 1992:

> I found Rukeiya and her six small children huddled in the corner of a dark, dank apartment not far from my well-manicured neighborhood in North Dallas. Other than the bundles she carried from her previous home in a Turkish mountain camp she had received only a few mattresses, eight dishes and spoons, and a single set of small American cooking pots. . . . [Her] husband, Ahmed, was taken by public transportation to a minimum wage night job, where he cleaned buses. As the family had been registered for food stamps and the children enrolled at school, the sponsoring agency closed its file.

Although life as a refugee is rarely easy, for many Middle Eastern refugees, the hardships are an improvement over the dangers they faced or the persecution they suffered in their own country. In several Middle Eastern Muslim countries, Christians can be imprisoned, forced into slavery, or killed for their beliefs. Seeking refugee status, not an easy process to begin with, has been more difficult under U.S. procedures instituted after the terrorist attacks of September 11, 2001. Many refugees remain in refugee camps more than a year after having been approved for refugee status in the United States.

Refugees in Canada

Canada's Immigration and Refugee Protection Act of 2002 enables people to be given refugee status through a resettlement program, in which they are brought from other countries and have Canadian government assistance or private sponsors; or, for individuals already in the country, through a refugee claim process. In 2014, Canada accepted 22,200 new refugees. Once they have lived in the country for three years, refugees can apply for Canadian citizenship.

 # Text-Dependent Questions

1. What spurred the "Lost Boys" of Sudan to leave their country?

2. Approximately how many undocumented immigrants were estimated to be in the United States in 2016?

3. How many refugees did the United States accept in 2014? How many refugees did Canada accept that same year?

 # Research Project

A wave of Iranians immigrated to North America after the Islamic Revolution of 1979. Research the causes and the results of that revolution. Organize your findings in an outline. Then use that outline to write a brief essay.

7 AN UNCERTAIN FUTURE

iddle Easterners have been immigrating to the United States for more than a century. In 2013, using data from the U.S. Census Bureau, the Migration Policy Institute estimated that there were about a million Middle Eastern immigrants in the country.

In the coming decades, immigration is expected to drive U.S. population growth. By 2065, the Pew Research Center projects, immigrants will make up 18 percent of the U.S. population (up from about 14 percent in 2015). Experts anticipate that new-comers from the Middle East will continue to arrive in signifi-cant numbers. But unforeseen developments could change that.

Historically, U.S. immigration policy (and the treatment of certain ethnic groups) has been shaped by world events. In the aftermath of World War I, for example, an increas-ingly isolationist United States shut its doors to many immi-grants with the development and passage of the Immigration Act of 1924, which imposed strict numerical quotas on certain nationalities. During the Great Depression, immigration was further limited when the State Department ordered consular officials to deny visas to all prospective immigrants who might at any time be unable to support themselves. After Japan's

◀ After more than a century of immigration to Canada and the United States, Middle Easterners have become an integral part of multicultural North America.

bombing of the U.S. naval base at Pearl Harbor, Hawaii, in December 1941, thousands of Japanese Americans on the West Coast were removed from their homes and taken to internment camps. More recently, some of the immigration reforms enacted in response to the September 11 terrorist attacks, such as the registration of men from certain countries, directly affected Middle Easterners.

A Few Scenarios

If another large-scale terrorist attack sponsored by an Islamist group occurred on U.S. soil, that would certainly affect public opinion, and it would probably influence public policy. Most likely, Middle Easterners would have a more difficult time rejoining family members who had already immigrated, earning a college degree in the United States, or pursuing the American Dream.

Another development that might have a potentially major effect on Middle Eastern immigration to the United States would be the resolution of the Israeli-Palestinian conflict and the establishment of an independent Palestinian state. Various American presidential administrations, Democratic and Republican alike, have tried to broker a peace agreement between Israel and the Palestinians. But none of these efforts has succeeded, and in recent years the prospects for an Israeli-Palestinian accord appear to have diminished.

If a Palestinian state were created, however, the result might well be a significant reduction in the number of Palestinians

 Words to Understand in This Chapter

isolationist—advocating or characteristic of a policy of avoidance of involvement in international affairs.

prospective—likely to come about; relating to or effective in the future.

scenario—an account or summary of a possible course of action or set of events.

An Arab Canadian family holds signs at Toronto's Pearson International Airport welcoming the first Syrian refugees to Canada, December 2015.

seeking to immigrate to North America. In addition, just as Jews from all over the world flocked to Israel following the creation of the Jewish state in 1948, many Palestinians living abroad—including those in Canada and the United States—might leave to help build up the new country.

Consider some other scenarios. What if the Berber language and culture were able to flourish in Algeria, where Berbers seeking to retain their traditions have been at the center of recurring civil unrest? Or if the Coptic Christians were no longer discriminated against in Egypt? It's possible these people would still come to North America to be reunited with family or go to college. But the push factors of migration would almost certainly be diminished, resulting in fewer immigrants from that part of the world.

For some Middle Easterners, the doors to North America might already be closing. For example, aside from asylum and refugee claims and the Diversity Lottery (which is at best a long shot), few options are available to the Sudanese, as Rogaia Mustafa Abusharaf explains. "Entering the United States is extremely difficult, especially since the closing of the American and Canadian consulates in Khartoum," she notes. "This difficulty is likely to persist."

Even Canada, which has earned a reputation as a haven for immigrants, might not be as welcoming in the future. A 2013 survey conducted by the Angus Reid Institute, a Canadian public opinion research organization, found 54 percent of Canadians holding an unfavorable view of Islam. A 2015 poll by EKOS Research Associates found that the proportion of Canadians opposed to immigration had nearly doubled over the

 ## A Rainbow After a Storm

The days and weeks after September 11, 2001, were frightening for all Americans, but uniquely for foreign-born Arab Muslim Americans. The possibility of hate crimes and the U.S. government's registration requirement for men from Muslim countries generated tremendous concern. But like a rainbow after a storm, a hope for better understanding of Muslim Americans has emerged at one Maryland college.

After 9/11, Hoda Zaki, an Egyptian immigrant and a political science professor at Hood College, found herself in an unusual situation. She was a nominal Muslim who identified more as an Arab American and a person of color than as a follower of Islam. In fact, Zaki came to the United States to pursue a master's degree at a traditionally African American college. "The Arab Americans I knew were part of an 'invisible' community that tried to blend in with the mainstream. I distanced myself from them, but connected with the African American community, where I felt welcome," says Zaki, director of Hood's African American Studies program.

Then came 9/11 and its aftermath. "The college was holding an inter-denominational prayer service, and the chaplain asked if I would read from the Koran," says Zaki. "I was unsure at first, as being Muslim was not a strong part of my identity, but being Arab American was."

Nonetheless, Zaki took part in the service. Her participation led a small, previously non-vocal group of international Muslim students to ask her if she'd be the adviser for a newly formed Muslim Student Association. She said yes, and the result was a student organization that opened new channels of communication at Hood College. "I'm heartened by this movement, by which the entire campus has been enriched," said Zaki.

previous decade. In 2015, according to the poll, 46 percent of Canadians thought their country was accepting too many immigrants overall; 41 percent said too many "visible minority" immigrants, including Arabs, were entering the country.

To varying degrees, the number of people coming to North America from the Middle East has continued to increase since U.S. and Canadian immigration laws changed in the 1960s. (One notable exception: Because of the Islamic Revolution in 1979, immigration from Iran dramatically spiked during the 1980s, but then dropped to only slightly above pre-revolution levels the following decade.)

The course of Middle Eastern immigration is difficult to predict. The fight against terrorism, U.S. immigration policy, and the prospects for peace in the region all will affect the outlook for future immigration from the Middle East.

 Text-Dependent Questions

1. Approximately how many Middle Eastern immigrants did the Migration Policy Institute estimate were living in the United States in 2013?

2. What effect did the U.S. Immigration Act of 1924 have?

3. How might an Israeli-Palestinian peace agreement affect Palestinian migration?

 Research Project

To become a U.S. citizen, an immigrant from another country must pass a civics test. U.S. Citizenship and Immigration Services offers practice tests at: https://my.uscis.gov/prep/test/civics/view
Take a test. What percentage did you get correct? Do some further research about any answers you got wrong.

Famous Middle Eastern Immigrants

Middle Easterners have been coming to North America since the late 1800s, so there are many famous Americans today who claim that heritage: Spencer Abraham, George W. Bush's secretary of energy; football player Doug Flutie; the founder of Mothers Against Drunk Driving, Candy Lightner; the founder of Kinko's copying stores, Paul Orfalea; rock legend Frank Zappa; actor Tony Shalhoub; poet Naomi Shihab Nye; consumer advocate and activist Ralph Nader; and many more. Listed below are some well-known Middle Eastern immigrants who have come to North America since 1965.

JOHN ABIZAID (1951–), a retired four-star army general who headed the U.S. Central Command, is of Lebanese heritage.

CHRISTIANE AMANPOUR (1958–) is a journalist and television anchor who was raised in Tehran, Iran, by her Iranian father and British mother. Amanpour is a naturalized U.S. citizen.

AMIN BARAKAT, who received the Ellis Island Medal of Honor in 2000, is a world-renowned pediatrician. The doctor and his family immigrated in 1986 because of the civil war in Lebanon.

MANUTE BOL (1963–2010), an NBA basketball player for 11 years and a Sudanese Dinka tribesman, Bol returned to Sudan for a few years but has come back to the United States. He established the Ring True Foundation to help Sudan's "Lost Boys."

THE IRON SHEIK (1942–), wrestler. An Olympic gold medalist in wrestling while representing Iran, the Iron Sheik (birth name: Khosrow Vaziri) came to the United States in 1970. For many years he was one of the World Wrestling Foundation's stars.

FAWAZ ISMAIL (1961–), entrepreneur. Ismail, who is of Palestinian descent, is the founder and president of Alamo Flag Company. The company is the largest distributor of American flags in the United States. He immigrated to the United States when he was nine years old.

STEVE JOBS (1955–2011), an inventor and entrepreneur, cofounded Apple Inc. Jobs's father was Syrian.

SAM KATZ (1951–) is a businessman and politician who served as mayor of Winnipeg. Katz, who was born in Israel, immigrated to Canada with his parents.

KRISTINA MARIA (1989–), a Canadian singer-songwriter of Lebanese extraction, was born Kristina Maria Chalhoub in Ottawa.

BIJAN MORTAZAVI (1957–), violinist. Born in Iran, the versatile musician attended college at Texas State University in 1979 and settled in California in 1985. Mortazavi has performed in concert halls worldwide, including New York's Lincoln Center.

RALPH NADER (1934–), the son of immigrants from Lebanon, is a political activist and four-time candidate for president of the United States.

MEHMET ÖZ (1960–), a surgeon and TV personality known to millions of viewers as Dr. Oz, was born in Cleveland to immigrants from Turkey.

NATALIE PORTMAN (1981–), born Neta-Lee Hershlag in Jerusalem, is an Academy Award–winning actress who has starred in three Star Wars films, Black Swan (2011), and other major motion pictures.

EDWARD SAID (1935–2003), a Palestinian American literary theorist, critic, and scholar, is perhaps best known for his 1978 book Orientalism.

AHMED HASSAN ZEWAIL (1946–), an immigrant to the United States from Egypt, won the 1999 Nobel Prize in Chemistry.

Series Glossary of Key Terms

assimilate—to adopt the ways of another culture; to fully become part of a different country or society.

census—an official count of a country's population.

deport—to forcibly remove someone from a country, usually back to his or her native land.

green card—a document that denotes lawful permanent resident status in the United States.

migrant laborer—an agricultural worker who travels from region to region, taking on short-term jobs.

naturalization—the act of granting a foreign-born person citizenship.

passport—a paper or book that identifies the holder as the citizen of a country; usually required for traveling to or through other foreign lands.

undocumented immigrant—a person who enters a country without official authorization; sometimes referred to as an "illegal immigrant."

visa—official authorization that permits arrival at a port of entry but does not guarantee admission into the United States.

Further Reading

Bourke, Dale Hanson. *Immigration: Tough Questions, Direct Answers.* Downers Grove, IL: InterVarsity Press, 2014.

Chomsky, Aviva. *Undocumented: How Immigration Became Illegal.* Boston: Beacon Press, 2014.

Gjelten, Tom. *A Nation of Nations: A Great American Immigration Story.* New York: Simon and Schuster, 2015.

Malek, Alia. *A Country Called Amreeka: U.S. History Retold Through Arab-American Lives.* New York: Free Press, 2009.

Merino, Noel. *Illegal Immigration.* San Diego: Greenhaven Press, 2015.

Said, Najla. *Looking for Palestine: Growing Up Confused in an Arab-American Family.* New York: Riverhead Books, 2013.

Stern, Jessica, and J. M. Berger. *ISIS: The State of Terror.* New York: HarperCollins, 2015.

Internet Resources

www.aaiusa.org

Since 1985 the Arab American Institute has encouraged political and civic participation by Americans of Arab descent and served as a clearinghouse of information about the Arab American community. This site provides demographic and census information about Arab Americans and tackles the hot policy issues surrounding the community.

www.islamonline.net

A comprehensive source about Islam, this site includes relevant articles about health and science, art and entertainment, and other contemporary issues. It is designed for non-Muslims as well as Muslims.

www.lexicorient.com/e.o/

From Abadan to Zurvanism, the Encyclopedia of the Orient has a wealth of information about North Africa and the Middle East.

www.niacouncil.org/

The website of the National Iranian American Council (NIAC) offers news and analysis, resources for students, and more.

www.arabamericanmuseum.org/

The home page of the Arab American National Museum.

www.caf.ca/

News, position papers, and more from the Canadian Arab Federation.

Index

Numbers in **bold italic** refer to captions.

Contributors

Senior consulting editor STUART ANDERSON is an adjunct scholar at the Cato Institute and executive director of the National Foundation for American Policy. From August 2001 to January 2003, he served as executive associate commissioner for Policy and Planning and Counselor to the Commissioner at the Immigration and Naturalization Service. He spent four and a half years on Capitol Hill on the Senate Immigration Subcommittee, first for Senator Spencer Abraham and then as Staff Director of the subcommittee for Senator Sam Brownback. Prior to that, Stuart was Director of Trade and Immigration Studies at the Cato Institute, where he produced reports on the military contributions of immigrants and the role of immigrants in high technology. Stuart has published articles in the Wall Street Journal, New York Times, Los Angeles Times, and other publications. He has an M.A. from Georgetown University and a B.A. in Political Science from Drew University. His articles have appeared in such publications as the *Wall Street Journal*, *New York Times*, and *Los Angeles Times*.

MARIAN L. SMITH served as the senior historian of the U.S. Immigration and Naturalization Service (INS) from 1988 to 2003, and is currently the immigration and naturalization historian within the Department of Homeland Security in Washington, D.C. She studies, publishes, and speaks on the history of the immigration agency and is active in the management of official 20th-century immigration records.

PETER HAMMERSCHMIDT is director general of national cyber security at Public Safety Canada. He previously served as First Secretary (Financial and Military Affairs) for the Permanent Mission of Canada to the United Nations. Before taking this position, he was a ministerial speechwriter and policy specialist for the Department of National Defence in Ottawa. Prior to joining the public service, he served as the Publications Director for the Canadian Institute of Strategic Studies in Toronto. He has a B.A. (Honours) in Political Studies from Queen's University, and an MScEcon in Strategic Studies from the University of Wales, Aberystwyth.

ED WARMS is a freelance writer and editor. He lives in New York City with his wife and two children. This is his first book.

Picture Credits